W0081791

THE DANGER FILES

REAL-LIFE DISASTERS

THE DANGER FILES

REAL-LIFE DISASTERS

ANNA CROWLEY REDDING

ILLUSTRATED BY
ROBBIE CATHRO

CANDLEWICK PRESS

Text copyright © 2025 by Anna Crowley Redding
Illustrations copyright © 2025 by Robbie Cathro

All rights reserved. No part of this book may be reproduced, transmitted,
or stored in an information retrieval system in any form or by any means,
graphic, electronic, or mechanical, including photocopying, taping, and
recording, without prior written permission from the publisher.

First edition 2025

Library of Congress Catalog Card Number 2023945070
ISBN 978-1-5362-1341-6 (hardcover)
ISBN 978-1-5362-3673-6 (paperback)

25 26 27 28 29 30 LEO 10 9 8 7 6 5 4 3 2 1

Printed in Heshan, Guangdong, China

This book was typeset in Miju Goudy.
The illustrations were created digitally.

Candlewick Press
99 Dover Street
Somerville, Massachusetts 02144

www.candlewick.com

EU Authorized Representative: HackettFlynn Ltd,
36 Cloch Choirneal, Balrothery, Co. Dublin, K32 C942, Ireland.
EU@walkerpublishinggroup.com

A JUNIOR LIBRARY GUILD SELECTION

To Quinn,
whose endless supply of fantastic questions
and love of disasters inspired this book
ACR

For Etain,
a friend who keeps stories
and history alive every day
RC

CONTENTS

YOUR MISSION!

DISASTERS, mysteries, disappearances, narrow escapes, and tales of survival. Experience some of the world's biggest catastrophes like never before. In this book, you get to play disaster detective!

You have access to the Danger Files, full of critical details about each event. You can dig through eyewitness accounts and fact files, conduct experiments, and follow the clues. Can you predict disaster before it happens? Can you figure out what is going wrong and why? Put your detective hat on—your investigation starts now!

FACT FILE
Chicago, Illinois
Founded: 1833
Population in 1871: 300,000 (fourth largest US city)
Nickname: The Gem of the Prairie
Location: Shores of Lake Michigan and the Chicago River

Chapter 1

THE GREAT CHICAGO FIRE

Chicago, Illinois

October 1–8, 1871

Chicago's firefighters were exhausted. Fire after fire. Grueling day after grueling day. They fought thick smoke and hot flames until their lungs ached with every tired, smoke-filled breath. There was no time to rest, as the alarm bell rang out nearly every hour with yet another blaze.

DANGER CLUE!

Fire needs three things to burn: fuel, heat, and oxygen. Fuel can be a liquid, a solid, or a gas. Examples include: wood, natural gas, coal, hay, paper, and much more. Types of heat: warm weather, sunlight, electricity, sparks, and friction. Oxygen: it's in the air all around us. In this case, Chicago had it all: plenty of fuel, warm weather, and strong, steady winds. The danger of fire was very high.

Everything was impossibly dry. It hadn't rained in months. And the long searing summer dragged on—into a hot autumn. Even the constantly blowing wind was warm. Chicago was normally muddy, wet, and much cooler in October. But now even creek beds evaporated into dusty ribbons of sand. The city's wooden buildings baked in the warm weather.

The firefighters were exhausted, but they had no idea that the fiercest fire of all was yet to come.

DANGER CLUE!

Chicago's usually muddy terrain made it a difficult city to get around in. That's why the city built 600 miles (966 kilometers) of raised wooden sidewalks and 55 miles (86 kilometers) of streets constructed out of pine planks.

Sunday, October 8, 1871

7:00 p.m.

EYEWITNESS

Name: Robert A. Williams

Born: June 25, 1827

Age: 44

Job: Chief fire marshal, City of Chicago

Uniform: Leather helmet; leather boots; coat, pants, and blazer made from thick wool, which is fire-resistant

---

Fire Chief Robert Williams was dead tired after sixteen hours of battling a fire at one of the city's lumber mills. The raging fire turned four city blocks into ruins. Finally, it was out and the chief could go home to get some sleep. Wearily, he hoisted one leg and then another into a horse-drawn wagon that would take him home.

The fire chief and his crew were worn out. Fatigue can make it a lot harder to carry out the strenuous tasks required to fight a fire. It also decreases a person's ability to make good decisions.

"We are going to have a burn," the worried chief said to his driver. "I feel it in my bones."

Even though he was worried about the night ahead, this was Chief Williams's chance to rest. Sinking into the mattress, he closed his reddened eyes and fell asleep.

FACT FILE
The O'Leary Residence
Address: 137 De Koven Street
Description: Wooden house with
separate barn

8:15 p.m.

In a Chicago neighborhood filled with Irish immigrants, Catherine O'Leary was settling in for the night. The cows had been milked, and the horse had been fed with a fresh supply of hay. Catherine and her husband, Patrick, tucked their five children into bed.

They had a lot to be thankful for. They had moved to the United States from Ireland for a better life. And things were going well. Not only did they own their house, it was also big enough to have a renter. In addition to rental money, Catherine sold the cows' milk and delivered it to her customers. Patrick earned what he could as a laborer. They were working toward a better future for their kids.

Soon enough, both parents fell asleep.

Ready for winter, the O'Learys' barn was filled with two tons (1.8 metric tons) of coal and two tons (1.8 metric tons) of hay. That's enough fuel to feed an intense fire.

8:35 p.m.

Just moments after the O'Learys settled into a deep slumber—horror! Black smoke gushed out of their barn. Neighbor and family friend Dan Sullivan saw it first. According to his testimony later, he rushed to the barn and yanked open the doors. The hayloft was engulfed in flames. He yelled for help and tried to save the O'Learys' animals. Another neighbor heard his cries and raced toward the O'Learys' house.

Catherine and Patrick woke up to panicked screams.

"Fire! Fire! Fire!"

FACT FILE

Reporting a Fire: Street Call Boxes

Street call boxes, located throughout the city, were considered state-of-the-art technology. When a city resident pulled a lever in the box, a telegraph message, automatically including the location of the box, was sent via wires to the fire department, alerting them to the fire.

With the neighbors' help, the O'Learys worked to keep their house from catching fire. Friends picked up the furniture and carried it to safety. Neighbors filled buckets and tubs with water from fire hydrants to pour onto the O'Learys' house. The O'Leary children were moved to safety. The barn could not be saved: only a single calf escaped before the structure burned to the ground.

Irish immigrants built the O'Learys' crowded neighborhood. The lots were small. The houses were close together. They were constructed of wood—the cheapest building material. As we know, wood burns easily. When wooden houses are built so closely together, it is easy for fire to spread, especially in windy conditions. All it takes is an ember from one house to land on the roof of the house next door.

Downtown, high atop the courthouse tower, a fire watchman looked through a spyglass. His job? To alert the fire department at the first sign of fire. After scanning the horizon, he spotted smoke rising from the O'Learys' barn. But he wasn't worried because he figured the smoke was from the fire at the lumber mill. He knew that even though the flames were out, it was still smoldering.

DANGER CLUE!

A neighbor of the O'Learys ran to the closest street call box and asked the storekeeper in charge of it to pull the alarm. It is unclear if that alarm was actually activated. It would have automatically sent the fire's location to the fire department. But many people were unsure about how to operate the boxes, including how to tell if their message even went through.

9:00 p.m.

Leaping from roof to roof, the fire spread quickly, setting aflame two blocks of jam-packed houses. The strong wind pushed the blaze toward the heart of the city.

DANGER CLUE!

The fire department's equipment was in rough shape. Three fire engines weren't working. Hoses needed mending. That meant quickly extinguishing a fire would be very difficult.

DANGER CLUE!

The O'Learys' fire got a thirty-minute head start before the fire department arrived.

FACT FILE

Chicago Fire Department, 1871

Number of firefighters: 185 full-time

Chief Fire Marshal: Robert A. Williams

Equipment:

- 54 hose carts
- 48,000 feet (14,600 meters) of hose
- 17 steam-powered fire engines (Using steam power, each engine's hoses could spray 600 gallons [2,270 liters] of water a minute.)
- 4 hook-and-ladder trucks
- 11 alarm bells located throughout the city
- 88 horses

Smoke Color

Smoke color can reveal whether a fire just started, is in the middle of burning, or is near its end.

White smoke means there's a lot of moisture around the fire. It's actually more steam than smoke. White smoke can be produced when firefighters or rain showers soak flames with water. It's a good sign the fire is out or almost out. But in some cases, white smoke can mean that a fire is just beginning. When a fire starts, there may be plenty of moisture in or near the burning materials. As the fire heats up, the flames produce enough heat to evaporate that moisture into steam.

Black smoke, on the other hand, indicates an active fire with plenty of fuel to burn (such as wooden houses or a forest of trees). Burning oil also creates black smoke. Gray smoke means a fire is running out of fuel.

Firefighters can use these clues to decide how to respond to a fire and which part of the fire needs their attention the most.

Billowing black smoke could be seen from far away. Now the fire watchman had no doubt that the smoke was not from the earlier lumber mill fire. This was a new crisis, and it was bad. The chief needed to be alerted right away!

Chief Williams's wife woke him up with the startling news. He hopped out of bed, grabbed his uniform, and hurried to the scene.

Wood crackled, crashed, and collapsed. The roar of the flames was deafening. As the chief took command, it was hard for firefighters to hear him shout orders.

People poured out of their houses, yelling "Fire!" and carrying buckets of water. But they were no match for this spreading disaster. They needed to plan their escape, and fast! The fire was gaining strength, and every second counted for anyone who needed a way to safety.

In 1871, Chicago had 59,500 buildings. Most were built completely out of wood.

Chief Williams called for more firefighters and more engines. The horse-drawn engines raced through the streets. Steam engines pumped water onto the blaze. The brutal heat made it nearly unbearable for firefighters to do their job.

Dousing the flames with thousands of gallons of water brought the fire under control. But just then, some of the fire hoses gave out. The fire reacted quickly. The intense heat flared. A whoosh of warm wind blew a fresh supply of oxygen onto the fire, giving it new life. The firefighters ran for their lives, leaving a vital hose behind. With no water to hold the fire back, a wall of flames began its push through the city.

The wind carried burning wooden cinders with it. They ignited the lumberyards, sidewalk planks, wooden houses, church steeples, and factories. The endless supply of wood and the warm wind sent flames a hundred feet into the red sky.

The fire started in the southern part of the city. The warm wind was blowing from the southwest at 20 miles (32 kilometers) per hour. Some people said it felt like a gale-force wind. That meant the wind could blow some of the water away, creating a mist—which meant less water for the fire. Plus, we already know that the equipment pumping the water through the hoses and onto the fire wasn't working well and that leaky hoses needed mending. Firefighters were in big trouble.

EYEWITNESS

Name: Bessie Bradwell

Born: 1858

Age: 13

Hometown: Chicago, Illinois

Family: Father, James; mother, Myra; and brother, Thomas

Thirteen-year-old Bessie Bradwell couldn't believe her eyes. It looked like one of Chicago's winter snowstorms. Only instead of white swirling snowflakes, glowing red-hot embers fell from the sky.

Bessie and her father, Judge James Bradwell, had already escaped their home. Her mom, Myra, and brother had grabbed some belongings and rushed to Lake Michigan's shoreline for safety.

Bessie and her father wouldn't be far behind. They stopped by his law office to collect his most important law books. But now he needed to find a wagon to carry them all. That wouldn't be easy.

Bessie waited at the front door as her father disappeared into the chaos of the streets. Minute after minute passed. Bessie's father was nowhere to be seen. The churn of airborne embers grew thicker. The air baked ever hotter as the fire roared closer.

DANGER CLUE!

Long before this fire, the fire department asked the city for more firefighting equipment. But the city did not want to raise taxes to pay for it. They were afraid people and businesses would not want to come to Chicago if taxes were too high. It turns out that would have been a small price to pay to have the tools to put this fire out quickly.

Panic spread as the streets filled with wagons and loose animals ran wild. Some people dragged trunks filled with their belongings, and others wrapped singed blankets around their bodies to protect themselves from the falling embers. Many tried to escape with only the clothes on their backs.

The gridlocked traffic moved slowly. Sometimes it barely moved at all. The constant crush of the crowd made it hard for families to stay together. Jostled and pushed, moms and dads were separated from their kids. Children cried. Panicked parents searched for them.

Bessie knew she couldn't wait for her father any longer. But what to do?

Just then, she spotted some of her parents' friends, who shouted, "Come with us!"

This could be her only chance to survive. Grabbing their hands, Bessie fled with them.

Randolph Street
(more than 1 mile/1.6 kilometers north of the O'Learys')
10:30 p.m.

The fire spread before the chief's eyes. He called for every available firefighter and engine. The chief ordered urgent telegrams asking for help from neighboring towns.

The Chicago River was polluted with oil, grease, and other liquids from factories and industries. Oil and grease are highly flammable, perfect fuel for the fire.

The Chicago River itself caught fire and spread the flames along its banks to more sections of the city. Boats in the river caught on fire. The fire marched 400 feet (120 meters) across the river and quickly consumed more neighborhoods on the other side.

Many buildings were built to be fireproof. These buildings' facades or shells were made of brick or stone. But often, wood was used to build the interior walls, support beams, and floors. And some roofs featured wooden shingles and other flammable materials. If an ember landed on a roof, it could spark a fire that would burn the building from the inside out.

The fire spread to the gasworks, the hub that supplied natural gas to the whole city, including to its street lanterns. The giant holding tank exploded, and the city's lanterns went dark. The chief rushed to the scene, but then felt a rumble. For a second the earth itself seemed to rattle and sway right where he stood. *Boom!* Ammunition and other explosives at a nearby armory had blown up.

11:50 p.m.

Chief Williams raced to his own house before it went up in flames. He saved his wife just in time.

Monday, October 9, 1871
1:30 a.m.

CLANG! CLANG! Above the courthouse, the heavy bell swung back and forth, ringing out a constant alarm.

The mayor hurried to the courthouse to help manage the crisis. But when he arrived, the courthouse was on fire. What about the prisoners? They were locked in jail cells in the basement.

DANGER CLUE!

The courthouse's brass bell weighed 10,849 pounds (4,921 kilograms). That's heavier than two rhinos! The prisoners could be crushed by the bell if it fell. Often in fires, falling debris like pieces of a roof or a collapsing chimney can be deadly to people below.

Soon they would be trapped in the flames. The mayor issued an urgent order: *Release all prisoners from jail at once.*

Heavy iron keys jangled as the jailer unlocked the cells. "Run!" he shouted to the prisoners. Five stories above, the brass bell continued to swing back and forth, ringing loudly until—*crash!* Just as the prisoners escaped the burning building, the bell plunged all the way down through one floor, and another, and another until it slammed into the bottom floor, crushing the jail cells.

Meanwhile, Bessie Bradford clung closely to her parents' friends as they fled the fire. They had to make it over the State Street Bridge and then they would be safe.

FACT FILE EXPERIMENT

Does a Fire Need Oxygen?

With an adult's help, carefully light three tea light candles. Place a large Mason jar over one candle. Place a small glass over the second candle. Leave the third candle alone. Write down your observations. What happens to each flame? Why?

But when they got there, the wooden bridge was on fire! Filled with fear, Bessie had to make a decision: either run across the burning bridge with the couple to safety or stay put, with nowhere else to go. As Bessie looked back, flames engulfed the city. Then she turned to the bridge. Racing the flames, she and her parents' friends charged across.

As she ran, Bessie heard a man suddenly shout, "This is the end of Chicago!"

"No," she called out to the stranger. "No. She will rise again."

While Bessie wound her way around Chicago's city blocks to safety, her father had returned to his office only to discover that Bessie was gone. He'd hoped that she had run to the lakeshore. He made his way there and found his wife and son. But Bessie was not with them. He and his wife began to panic.

DANGER CLUE!

One man had an idea for stopping the fire: blowing up houses. If the fire ran out of wooden

structures, he figured, it would die out. He began
blowing up buildings, but no one would help him.
He could not destroy enough structures quickly
enough to stop the fire. Sometimes a similar
technique, called a controlled burn, is used in
fighting forest fires. But in Chicago, the tactic
could easily have backfired. The wind was so
strong that embers from the explosions could have
traveled and started more fires.

The fire hoses sputtered. Then nothing. Not a single drop of water. The waterworks building that pumped water out of the lake into hydrants and then into those hoses had caught fire, too. Now any hope of putting out the fire was gone. The fire department was out of options. Chief Williams watched the waterworks burn. He knew his fight was over. There was nothing more the fire department could do. The fire had won. The firefighters had lost.

Some fires become so intense they create their own wind. When a huge fire heats up the air around it, that air becomes less dense (or less heavy) and rises quickly. Sometimes the air rises so fast, it creates a vacuum. To fill the vacuum, the fire pulls in the surrounding air, creating a strong wind. This makes an intensely powerful fire called a firestorm.

A firestorm's pull can create a wind speed on the ground up to ten times faster than the wind that's naturally blowing as a part of regular weather! So if the wind in Chicago was blowing at 20 miles (32 kilometers) per hour, then a firestorm would have been capable of creating winds of up to 200 miles (320 kilometers) per hour. And if heated air rises fast enough, the spinning firestorm can turn into a fire tornado.

The hot wind blowing from the southwest to the northeast fanned the flames higher and higher, creating a firestorm. To the people fleeing, it felt like a hurricane.

Some of Chicago's residents were trapped, with no hope of escape. Others waded into Lake Michigan's cold waters to stay out of reach of the flames and the heat. Survivors had to wait as hour after hour the fire consumed more of the city.

DANGER CLUE!

Before this fire, the chief had asked for stricter building codes and more fire inspectors to enforce them. Improved codes would call for more space between buildings and other safety rules. The inspectors would check for fire hazards and be sure the codes were followed to reduce the risk of fire. But the city did not want to pay for them.

`9:00 p.m.`

Red embers weren't the only thing falling down from above. Rain started to fall. Then torrential showers. At last, enough water fell on the flames to put out the fire.

FACT FILE

Anti-immigrant, Anti-Catholic Prejudice

On Monday evening, as the city continued to burn, the *Chicago Evening Journal* put out a special edition. It reported that Mrs. O'Leary was milking her cow by lantern light right before the fire. The reporter who wrote the story said that the O'Learys' cow kicked the lantern and it exploded, causing the fire. This story played on anti-immigrant, anti-Catholic, and anti-Irish bigotry of the time. Irish immigrants were often judged as stupid, dirty, and poor. That made Mrs. O'Leary an easy scapegoat. And the story was quickly reprinted around the world.

But the truth is, the reporter made it up. While the fire did start in the O'Learys' barn, Catherine was inside her house, asleep, at the time. Years later, the reporter admitted to lying about Catherine and her cow. But the story followed her for the rest of her life.

October 10, 1871
4:00 a.m.

Thirty-one hours after the fire had started, it was finally over. One-third of the city, more than four square miles, was nothing more than ash and ruins. Block after block of smoldering rubble remained where grand hotels, government buildings, and beautiful shops once stood.

FACT FILE

The Damage

Total damage: $200 million (approximately $3 billion in today's dollars)

Deaths: About 300 people

Number of buildings destroyed: 18,000

Number left homeless: 100,000. Shelters were set up at churches and schools, and people opened their homes to survivors.

Aid: Help—in the form of money, equipment, clothes, food, and more—arrived from all over the world. Undamaged railroad tracks made it possible to get these donations into the city quickly. People in England collected and sent books—a donation that made it possible for Chicago to open its first public library.

Judge Bradwell had been searching for Bessie for hours. The fire was out, and she still hadn't been found. Her family didn't know if she had escaped.

The stench of a charcoaled city assaulted his nose as he trudged down the street to an emergency citizens' meeting—where many people were gathered who might be able to help him find Bessie.

There was so much to talk about. How to rebuild? How to feed the hungry? How to provide shelter for the homeless fire victims? But Judge Bradwell had one thing on his mind: his missing daughter. He raised his voice as he talked about Bessie and his search for her. Just then, a man who heard the judge jumped from his seat and said, "Don't worry, Judge Bradwell. Your daughter is safe."

It wasn't long before Bessie and Judge Bradwell were together again, safe and sound.

Not everyone was that lucky. About three hundred people died in the fire. And one hundred thousand people, nearly one-third of all Chicagoans, lost their homes.

One survivor said, "With the exception of a ten-dollar bill, which I happened to have in my pocketbook, I have lost every cent I ever had in the world."

FACT FILE

A Piece of History

The Chicago Historical Society held the original Emancipation Proclamation—the document that freed enslaved people during the Civil War in the states that rebelled against the Union. It was signed by Abraham Lincoln. The historical society's building did not survive the fire, and neither did that treasured document.

But as Bessie said so perfectly when she fled the fire, Chicago would rise again. Indeed, even before the ruins stopped smoldering, the people of Chicago began to clear the debris and rebuild.

But for Catherine O'Leary, who was wrongfully accused of starting the fire, life was never the same. While her house survived the fire, her reputation was ruined. A couple of days after the fire, she swore under oath that she did not start the fire, but her testimony was no match for rumor and bad reporting. It wasn't until 1997 that she was officially cleared of all blame, long after she had died. The exact cause of the fire has never been determined.

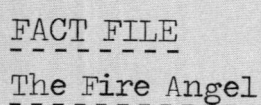

FACT FILE

The Fire Angel

Anna Elizabeth Hudlin

February 6, 1840–November 21, 1914

Anna Elizabeth Hudlin was desperate to help. Her beloved city of Chicago was on fire. The flames had not reached the small home she and her husband, Joseph, had worked so hard to build—making them the first Black couple in the whole city to build and own a home. She had to do something. People were injured. Some were lost. Some were homeless. So many in need.

Anna ran into the smoky streets and rushed over to help as many people as she could, guiding them into her home. She had enough room for five families. With only five rooms and five children of her own, it would be cramped. But they would all be safe there—as long as the fire didn't spread to her doorstep. Anna poured water for her guests and shared what food she had on hand.

The truth was that she knew what it was like to need help. Her own mother had been freed from slavery just in time to give birth to Anna. A baby girl born into freedom! Another family had stepped in to help raise Anna while her mother worked hard. Eventually they'd moved to Chicago.

As Anna took care of the fleeing families, Joseph risked his life to help his employer. He worked as a janitor at the Board of Trade building. Joseph headed toward the fire, then ran inside the building, opened the vault, and saved important papers before the building disappeared into the wall of flame.

When the fire stopped burning, Anna and Joseph invited the families they'd taken in to stay as long as they needed. For her heroism and selflessness, the community called Anna "the Fire Angel." Fire would strike Chicago again just three years later. Anna would once again rise to the challenge, providing food, a place to stay, and warm clothes.

IMPACT ⚡

Construction

Before the fire, Chicago had experienced a population boom. People moved there faster than locals could build houses for newcomers to live in, stores to shop in, or factories to work in. As a result, construction had been fast and cheap. The goal was getting the buildings built, not building them in a safe way that would prevent them from catching fire.

After the fire, building codes became stricter. Not only that, but the fire department was also able to hire more inspectors to check out buildings and enforce these codes. One rule? No more wooden buildings. This new rule changed the look of the city. Architects, engineers, and designers began to build with steel and concrete, which resulted in a new kind of building: skyscrapers. Terra-cotta was also used.

Soon, steel-framed skyscrapers began appearing in cities around the country and eventually around the world.

Fire Protection

After the fire, the city's fire department was able to reorganize and get lots of new equipment, boosting its firefighting power over the next thirty years. By 1900, it had five fireboats, more than one hundred fire engines, thirty-four hook-and-ladder trucks, and, amazingly, the number of firefighters had increased to 1,142!

Training and Education

Every year in the United States, Fire Prevention Week is observed around October 8; that's a nod to the terrible Chicago fire and the lessons learned from it.

The lot where the O'Learys lived and where the fire started is now owned by the fire department and used for training. Even today, no one knows exactly what started the Great Chicago Fire.

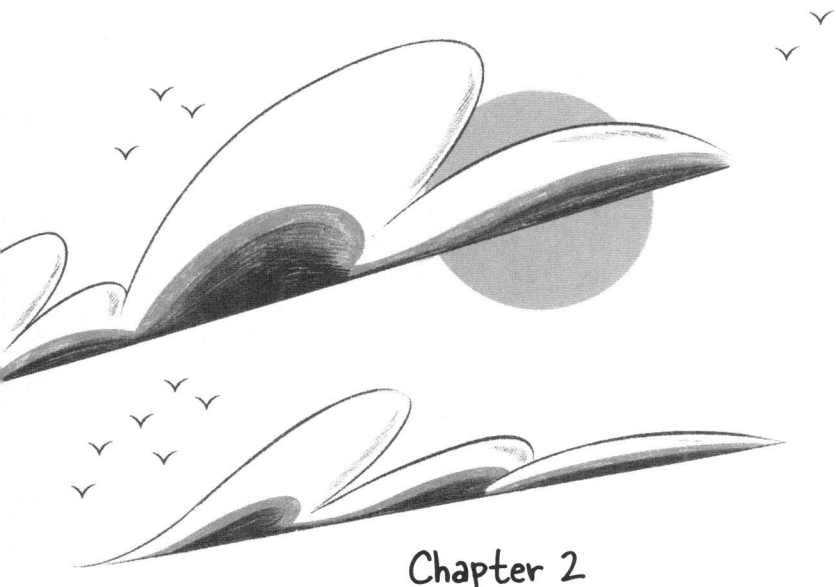

Chapter 2

TITANIC: SHIP OF DOOM

Whooooo-woooooo! With a burst of steam, the train whistled and chugged down the tracks. The black engine snaked along Southampton's seaside docks and rumbled to a stop. This wasn't just any train. This special train was reserved for lucky passengers about to take a voyage on a great ship.

EYEWITNESS

Name: Frankie Goldsmith

Born: December 19, 1902

Age: 9

Hometown: Kent, England

Family: Mother, Emily, and father, Frank

Destination: New York City, then Detroit, Michigan

Ticket: Third-class

Ticket price: $30

Jumping down the steps of the train, Frankie couldn't believe his eyes. The *Titanic* towered high above the cheering crowds. "Ticket, please!"

This was it. The start of Frankie's new life. Frankie and his parents were moving to America. They had talked about it for months: a fresh start in Detroit, where there would be jobs and opportunity. Frankie hoped there would be cowboys, too. Best of all—they were taking the *Titanic* to get there. What an adventure!

FACT FILE

Titanic

Owner: White Star Line

Builder: Harland and Wolff

Designer: Thomas Andrews

Captain: Edward John Smith

Weight: 52,310 tons (47,455 metric tons)

Length: 882 feet, 9 inches (269 meters)

Crew members: Approximately 900

DANGER CLUE!

Captain Smith embarked on a seafaring career at age thirteen with an apprenticeship. He had commanded naval ships. Then Smith joined White Star Line in 1880 and sailed their biggest ships. He often earned a bonus for his excellent performance. However, in 1899, a ship under his command capsized. Then in 1911, a ship under his command collided with a tugboat, and later that same year his ship smashed into another ship.

The *Titanic* was referred to in many ways: Unsinkable. A floating palace. A ship of dreams. As tall as an eleven-story building, as long as three football fields, *Titanic* was the largest ocean liner in the world. And it was the most talked about. No wonder! *Titanic* was filled with the finest furniture and the best-tasting food anyone could imagine.

A total of 2,214 people boarded the *Titanic* before it crossed the Atlantic. There were sixteen wooden lifeboats and four collapsible boats on board, with space for 1,178 people. The ship needed at least 1,036 more seats in lifeboats for everyone to have a seat.

First-class passengers had the most expensive tickets. They enjoyed the very finest luxuries and facilities on board the ship, from gourmet food to richly decorated parlors, a swimming pool, and a gymnasium. Every detail was designed to dazzle. The most impressive feature was a grand staircase that spiraled beneath an ornate glass dome.

FACT FILE

Titanic's Cargo

Bags of mail: 3,000

Butter: 6,000 pounds (2,700 kilograms)

Fish: 11,000 pounds (5,000 kilograms)

Potatoes: 40 tons (36 metric tons)

Flour: 200 barrels

Milk: 1,500 gallons (5,700 liters)

Meat: 75,000 pounds (34,000 kilograms)

Oranges: 36,000

Eggs: 40,000

Coffee: 2,200 pounds (1,000 kilograms)

Tea: 800 pounds (360 kilograms)

Miscellaneous: · 5 baby grand pianos
· 1 fancy car
· several dogs
· a pet pig

FACT FILE

Titanic's Construction

<u>Double bottom:</u> The hull of the ship had two layers, or a double bottom. If the ship collided with something, only the outer layer would be punctured. The inner layer would keep the ship from taking on water.

<u>Watertight compartments:</u> But what if somehow the inner layer was damaged and water came pouring in? Titanic's designers divided the belly of the ship into compartments separated by watertight walls. This way, any flooding into one compartment could be contained there rather than moving to flood further areas of the ship. At the time, this was cutting-edge design and engineering.

<u>Radio room:</u> Long before cell phones, ships needed a way to communicate with one another and to relay messages to land. Titanic had a state-of-the-art "radio room," where wireless telegraph operators worked sending and receiving messages using Morse code.

Second-class passengers were also treated to fine dining and great service, beautiful rooms, and a library. They could talk books over tea when it was served every afternoon. Third-class travelers paid the least for their tickets. Many of them were sailing to America for a better life because their home countries were not safe or didn't have enough jobs or opportunities for them to earn money to support their families. *Titanic* offered these passengers clean, safe accommodations with three meals a day. While enjoying nowhere near the luxury first-class passengers experienced, third-class travelers, like Frankie and his family, were impressed.

Not only was *Titanic* beautiful, but the ocean liner's builders and engineers had used brand-new technology and ideas to make her the safest ship on the seas. *Titanic* was ready for its first voyage. And nine-year-old Frankie was ready for adventure.

DANGER CLUE!

Remember those watertight walls? One problem:
the walls between these anti-flooding compartments
did not go all the way to the ceiling. There were big
gaps at the top of the walls! So they would only
keep out certain amounts of water and would work
best when the ship was level. This oversight would
make *Titanic's* watertight compartments useless if
water levels rose above the tops of the walls.

When the clock struck noon, Captain Edward Smith gave a signal. A loud whistle blasted three times. Five tugboats pushed the giant ship away from the docks. *Titanic*'s engines churned. Its smokestacks spewed. By the time the ship sailed out of port, Frankie had already made friends. He and his new gang raced up and down the hallways. They chased one another up the stairs and back down again.

Before leaving England, the crew aboard *Titanic* had conducted only one safety drill. Practicing what to do in an emergency gives everyone the best chance of making smart choices during a real crisis.

As third-class passengers, they could not explore the very fancy and fine parts of the ship. But they didn't care. After all, what good was a stroll on a gorgeous promenade when you could climb a cargo crane instead? Or better yet, spy on the stokers, trimmers, and greasers in the boiler room shoveling coal into *Titanic*'s gigantic boilers.

FACT FILE

Titanic Fuel

At the start of its voyage, *Titanic* carried 5,892 tons (5,345 metric tons) of coal. It took 690 tons (626 metric tons) of coal a day to run the ship's steam-powered engines.

TITANIC

DANGER CLUE!

The coal was stored in bunkers, which were giant metal bins—filled to capacity. Days before *Titanic* set sail, coal in one bunker caught fire and was still slowly burning. That meant the steel hull plates and bolts next to the fire were exposed to high heat for weeks, which weakened that section of the hull.

The ship picked up more passengers in France and in Ireland and then, on April 11, 1912, steamed toward New York.

DANGER CLUE!

Over the winter, Arctic weather had been warmer than usual, causing icebergs to break free from glaciers and float south into the paths of ships. In contrast, the weather in these shipping lanes had been colder than normal because of the icebergs. So once the icebergs arrived in the shipping lanes, they were less likely to melt than they would have been if there were fewer of them.

For the next few days, everyone settled into life aboard the ship. By day, Frankie listened to coal-dust-covered workers sing as they toiled. By night, tucked into bed, Frankie fell asleep to the hum of *Titanic*'s roaring engines.

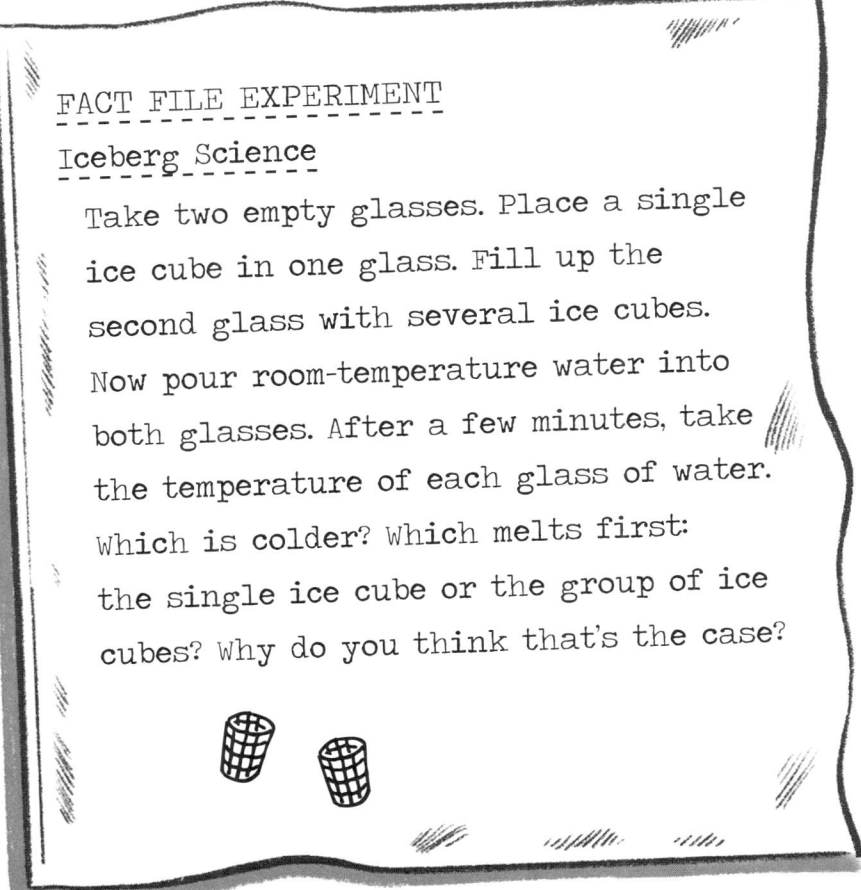

FACT FILE EXPERIMENT

Iceberg Science

Take two empty glasses. Place a single ice cube in one glass. Fill up the second glass with several ice cubes. Now pour room-temperature water into both glasses. After a few minutes, take the temperature of each glass of water. Which is colder? Which melts first: the single ice cube or the group of ice cubes? Why do you think that's the case?

Captain Smith had been increasing *Titanic*'s speed a little each day. *Titanic*'s owner, White Star, was in fierce competition with its competitor the Cunard Line. Both companies wanted to build the most luxurious ship, the biggest ship, and the fastest ship. The pressure was on to get to New York as quickly as possible. Going faster and faster meant that if *Titanic* hit an iceberg, it would do so with incredible force. The greater the speed, the greater the impact.

FACT FILE

Titanic's Speed and Distance Traveled

Fastest speed: 23 knots (26½ miles/ 43 kilometers per hour)

Distance traveled each day after leaving Europe:

Friday, April 12: 386 miles (621 kilometers)

Saturday, April 13: 519 miles (835 kilometers)

Sunday, April 14: 546 miles (879 kilometers)

By Sunday, the weather had turned bitter cold. The sea was calm. *Titanic* sailed full steam ahead— straight for an ice field.

DANGER CLUE!

The ice field measured about 30 nautical miles (35 miles/56 kilometers) by 15 nautical miles (17 miles/28 kilometers)—that's almost 400,000 acres (1,600 square kilometers), nearly double the size of New York City!

10:30 a.m.

As a special treat that first Sunday, the captain invited passengers from every class to join him in the first-class dining room for a prayer service. The orchestra played along as crew and passengers sang popular hymns.

DANGER CLUE!

Captain Smith canceled a lifeboat safety drill that was supposed to take place after the prayer service.

As the day went on, some passengers took a dip in the ship's swimming pool, others played cards or danced belowdecks to the sound of fiddles. Some of the wealthiest passengers wrote messages and took them to the radio room to be sent home. It was the height of wealth and fashion to use this new technology to send a personal message from the middle of the ocean. And to be able to send a message from *Titanic*'s maiden voyage, now, *that* was something.

.... .. / -- --- --*

* Hi Mom

Titanic Tech

Innovation: Morse code

Inventor: Samuel F. B. Morse

Born: Charlestown, Massachusetts, 1791

Morse code is an alphabetic code that allows you to spell out words and sentences by tapping a pattern of dots and dashes. Morse code messages traveled through telegraph wires that were strung up along railroad lines.

* * *

Innovation: Wireless telegraph

Inventor: Guglielmo Marconi

Born: Bologna, Italy, 1874

Marconi learned Morse code and figured out how to send coded messages using wireless radio waves. He was the first to send a message from a ship back to land. The telegraph machine aboard the *Titanic* was made by Marconi's company, and the operators worked for him. This was cutting-edge technology. Just as runners in a relay race pass a baton, ships could wirelessly pass messages to each other until they reached onshore operators.

The radio was also an important safety feature for relaying messages about conditions in the shipping lane. As the passengers relaxed, the radio operators were getting multiple ice warnings. *Icebergs and large quantities of field ice in 41°51′ N, 40°52′ W.* The operators handed the warning to the captain. The captain passed the note to the chairman of White Star Line, J. Bruce Ismay. Ismay took the warning and stuffed it in his pocket.

Back in the radio room: disaster! Around lunchtime, the telegraph machine stopped working. The stack of messages to be sent was piling up.

The operators tinkered with the circuits for hours to solve the problem.

Finally, after seven hours, a fix! The telegraph machine was working again. Now the operators not only had a huge number of messages to send, but they also had many to receive. They were very busy.

DANGER CLUE!

Wireless radio signals grow weaker the farther they have to travel. *Titanic* was sending and receiving messages directly to a telegraph station in Nova Scotia, which was 800 miles (1,300 kilometers) away. Weak signals were difficult to hear—like when you are in a room full of people talking and someone from another room speaks and it's very difficult to hear them. Meanwhile, the messages sent and received by nearby ships were stronger and louder. Ship radio operators often made silly chitchat over the telegraph to pass the time, which interrupted *Titanic*'s operators as they tried to catch up. When you are focused, you respond better to a crisis.

The temperature continued to drop, and the ice warnings continued to come in. The most serious warning told of large icebergs just south of the ship the *Californian*. But Captain Smith was busy talking to passengers at dinner. No one gave him the message. *Titanic* reached its top speed so far, averaging 22½ knots (nearly 26 miles/42 kilometers per hour).

While passengers went to sleep, two lookouts climbed into *Titanic*'s crow's nest. Their job? To spot dangerous icebergs. But that night, the work was really difficult. The moonless night made it extra dark.

DANGER CLUE!

The lookouts' binoculars had gone missing. A magnified view would have allowed lookouts to see faraway objects more quickly, giving them more time to react. They were forced to rely solely on their unassisted eyes.

11:00 p.m.

Another ice warning arrived from the *Californian*. They were blocked in by ice. Meanwhile, *Titanic*'s radio operator was still desperately trying to catch up sending and receiving messages. His response to the *Californian*? Shut up.

DANGER CLUE!

Early ice warnings via telegraph were important so that ships could slow down and change course.

Other than the hum of the engines and the tapping of radio messages, *Titanic* had grown quiet. Lights were dimmed. It was time for a good night's rest. Deep in the ship, Frankie was tucked into his bed and had already been asleep for quite some time. His mom and dad were also fast asleep.

DANGER CLUE!

When seas are rough, waves break against icebergs, which makes it easier to spot them. But this night, the seas were dead calm.

Up in the crow's nest, one of the lookouts spotted something. A dark shadow appeared, growing larger as *Titanic* sailed closer. Suddenly the lookout knew exactly what it was.

"Iceberg right ahead!"

DANGER CLUE!

The iceberg was about a mile (1.6 kilometers) away when the lookouts saw it. The ship was traveling at an average of 22½ knots, or 26 miles (42 kilometers) per hour. While the iceberg towered high above the water, the largest part of it was hidden beneath the surface. If *Titanic's* crew had had binoculars in the crow's nest, they might have spotted the iceberg sooner, slowed the ship, and made the turn in time to avoid the iceberg.

The lookout rang the alarm bell three times. Down below, the first officer tried to slow the ship. He tried to steer away from danger. But it was no use.

DANGER CLUE!

The double hull reinforced only the bottom of the ship. The sides of the great ship featured a single-layer hull. The double bottom protected the belly of the ship from icebergs, but the single layer on the sides made the ship vulnerable to side impacts.

11:40 p.m.

Titanic struck the iceberg. The ice sliced the side of the ship just below the waterline, cutting the ship's hull. Water poured in.

DANGER CLUE!

Decades later, tests on *Titanic*'s steel hull and rivets showed that the material used was poor quality and easily failed in cold water. Additionally, exposing metal to extreme temperatures—like from the coal fire and then the frigid water— makes metal brittle. Weakened steel is no match for the sharp, razor-like scraping of an iceberg.

The engines stopped.

Frankie woke up to his mother dressing him. The hum of the engines had been replaced by silence. Then there was a knock at the door. It was the ship's doctor. He asked Frankie's mom if they had life vests and he told her to put them on and head for the lifeboats.

FACT FILE
Life Vests

The life vests on the *Titanic* were constructed of cork panels covered in canvas. There were enough for every passenger, but they were fairly flimsy. And they could not protect people from the cold. Many passengers put them on over their heavy winter coats.

Frankie wasn't scared. Already he'd had such an amazing time aboard *Titanic*. He and his friends had seen the lifeboats. And now to be allowed on one? *What an adventure!* Frankie thought. Grabbing a handful of candy, Frankie followed his mother and father out the door.

12:15 a.m.

The captain commanded the radio operators to send out the first call for help, a distress call. The operators carefully tapped out the code CQD, which the Marconi company used as an international signal of distress or serious emergency. But then *Titanic* also sent out the newer call for help, SOS.

Other ships could have heard *Titanic* call for help, but some radio operators aboard those ships were already in bed for the night.

12:25 a.m.

The captain realized that *Titanic* was going to sink.

As the ship's crew shouted orders, Frankie and his family hustled down the hallway, clambered up a staircase, raced across the promenade deck, and climbed more stairs—until a guard stopped them at a gate.

Like many of *Titanic*'s travelers, this was the moment when they discovered there were not enough lifeboats for everyone.

The guard would not let men pass through the gate, only women and children.

Frankie's father hugged him. "So long, Frankie. I'll see you later." Frankie watched as his mother and father embraced. Then his mother took him by the hand. They had to make it to a lifeboat. Time was running out.

FACT FILE

Calling *Carpathia*

Owned by: Cunard Line

Time they received *Titanic*'s distress calls: April 15, 12:20 a.m.

Distance from *Titanic*: 58 miles (93 kilometers)

Travel time: about 3 hours

Hundreds of people were still on board. *Titanic* needed help, and fast!

Titanic's crew shot emergency rockets into the sky, hoping a nearby ship would see them. *Titanic*'s radio operators continued to send out calls for help.

An optical illusion was brewing on the horizon. The horizon appeared higher than its actual location. If you were standing on *Titanic*'s deck, searching the horizon for an iceberg, it would have been hidden from view by a mirage. For nearby ships searching for the enormous ship, it would also have been hard to spot because the false horizon would have made the ship look so small that it couldn't possibly be the *Titanic*.

This effect was caused by light refraction, or bending of light, called thermal inversion. When you see an object, your eyes are receiving light. But certain weather conditions can bend light on its way to your eyes, as when warm air traps cold air beneath it, forming layers. When light travels through the layers, it is bent. This bending can make the horizon appear much higher than it actually is. Imagine looking out at the ocean and thinking that you are seeing where the sea meets the sky, but actually, it's a trick of light. The real horizon is several feet lower. But you can't see it!

Meanwhile, Frankie and his mom scrambled to a steel ladder. Grabbing the cold metal rungs, Frankie pulled himself up. *Clang! Clang!* Frankie climbed all the way to the top. But when he and his mom arrived on the boat deck, most of the lifeboats were gone!

In the panic, lifeboats were lowered quickly, even before every seat was filled. While there was space for 1,178 people to escape, that's only if every seat was used.

Looking ahead, just past the smokestack funnel, Frankie's mother spotted a lifeboat. Suddenly a man jumped in front of Frankie, blocking his way. Frankie felt his mother let go of his hand just long enough for her to push the man out of the way. She gripped Frankie's hand again, and together, they climbed into the boat.

"Lower away!" Their lifeboat jerked and lurched toward the black water.

Overhead, a phenomenon called the northern lights, or aurora borealis, swirled with vibrant colors. This light occurs when solar flares hit Earth's atmosphere, causing a geomagnetic storm. The storms can wreak havoc on radio waves, disrupting the signals. *Titanic*'s radio operators continued to frantically send messages to other ships, but many of those ships reported later that they did not receive the messages.

Klush. Klush. The women pushed their oars into the icy sea and rowed away in the last lifeboats to escape *Titanic.*

As water flooded the ship, *Titanic's* bow was pulled under the sea. Suddenly there was an explosion. The magnificent ship broke in two. Frankie's mother reached for him and hugged him tight so he could not see what happened next.

DANGER CLUE!

Multiple watertight compartments were sliced by the iceberg and filled with water. The weight of the water dragged the ship down.

2:20 a.m.

Titanic sank two and a half miles (four kilometers) to the bottom of the ocean. Many of the passengers who were still on board fell into the water.

"Help! Help!" they cried. But the lifeboats pulled only forty people from the icy water. Those cries grew quieter and quieter. And then they stopped.

DANGER CLUE!

The ocean's temperature that night, 28°F (-2°C), would make it nearly impossible for people in the water to survive more than fifteen or twenty minutes.

Survivors in the lifeboats hoped help would come. The wait was cold and scary.

3:35 a.m.

They heard a ship in the distance. The *Carpathia* was arriving to save them!

Frankie stepped into a burlap mail sack and was hoisted up to safety aboard the ship. He and his mother were safe. Once aboard the *Carpathia*, Frankie's mother gathered blankets, thread, needles, and scissors and began sewing new, dry clothes for *Titanic*'s children.

Thursday, April 18, 1912

Under storm clouds and rain, the *Carpathia* steamed into New York Harbor. Once they were ashore, survivors began to tell the story of the "unsinkable" *Titanic*, the floating palace, the ship of dreams—and how those dreams had ended in disaster.

Like so many other male passengers, Frankie's father died when the ship went down. But Frankie went on to live a long life, marrying, having children and grandchildren. Frankie's last wish was to be buried at sea on the very spot where *Titanic* sank.

On April 15, 1982, the US Coast Guard granted Frankie's wish. As a Coast Guard plane circled above the area where *Titanic* went down, a hatch door opened. Coast Guardsmen released a memorial wreath for those lost. And they also released Frankie's ashes to the sea.

FACT FILE

Tragedy by the Numbers

Number of people who survived: 705

Number who died: 1,496

Survival by class:

First class: 200

Second class: 117

Third class: 172

Crew, staff, and servers: 216

IMPACT ⚡

Ice Patrol

The *Titanic*'s sinking forever changed the way ships cross that part of the Atlantic Ocean. The International Ice Patrol prowls the North Atlantic, looking for icebergs. They send warnings to nearby ships to prevent collisions.

Lifeboats

Ships are now required to have enough lifeboats to save every person on board.

On Duty

Radio operators now have dedicated channels to discuss all safety matters. Safety communications became the priority. And no sleeping on the job! Radio operators work in shifts; an operator has to be present in the radio room twenty-four hours a day.

Wreck Discovery

In 1985, undersea explorer Robert Ballard located *Titanic*'s wreck site and filmed what was left of the ship. For the first time in seventy years, people were able to see *Titanic*. Today, the shipwreck is slowly disappearing. Water currents carrying sand are burying part of the site. And tiny bacteria and fungi are eating away the iron and steel. Many objects from *Titanic* have been brought up from the bottom of the ocean, from teacups to jewelry to a huge section of *Titanic*'s hull. Some of these objects are on display at museums and as a traveling exhibit.

Chapter 3

THE SPANISH FLU

EYEWITNESS

Name: Irven Armstrong

Born: March 7, 1892

Age: 26

Hometown: Indianapolis, Indiana

Job: Middle-school teacher

Irven Armstrong stood in front of the chalkboard, ready to write another equation for his attentive students. He looked out at his class—a sea of beautiful Black faces and bright minds. He'd spend part of his weekend cleaning the chalkboard, decorating the classroom, and putting up the week's poems. He wanted his room to inspire. That's what Irven loved most about his job, sparking a love of learning in his students.

Even though Irven loved teaching, his attention was being pulled in another direction: World War I. Democracy and freedom were at risk. And as the son of a formerly enslaved man, Irven devoted himself not only to the cause of freedom and democracy, but to the fight for equality, too. Irven's dad had escaped slavery by fighting for the Union in the Civil War.

For Irven, the call of war could not be ignored. Irven and his four brothers joined the army.

Segregation

In 1918, the United States was segregated. Black students went to one school, and white students went to another. That was the law. Irven taught at Public School No. 17, a school for Black students. Irven's students faced the same obstacle he did: racism. That was a devastating reality.

Years earlier, as a teenager, Irven had been the only Black student allowed to study at an all-white high school. And he had studied hard to become the valedictorian of his class. Having achieved the highest grades of all his classmates, he was supposed to walk at the front of the line at graduation. But his teacher said that because he was Black, he had to go last. Irven refused and walked in the middle of the line instead.

DANGER CLUE!

Many of America's nurses and doctors were sent to Europe to take care of wounded soldiers. That helped the war effort but meant that hospitals at home were not fully staffed.

Before he headed off to war, Irven made his students a promise. He would write them letters to let them know how he was doing. Irven hoped they would write back.

He traveled across the country, boarded a ship to France, and joined the war. It wasn't long before he was promoted to sergeant. While soldiers focused on fighting, they had no idea that they would also soon battle an additional enemy: influenza.

FACT FILE

World War I

Also known as the Great War

Years: 1914–1918

Combatants: The Allies (United States, Great Britain, Belgium, France, Russia, Italy, Romania, and Japan) versus the Central Powers (Germany, Austria-Hungary, the Ottoman Empire, and Bulgaria)

Number of military personnel readied for war: 70 million worldwide

Number of deaths: 16-18 million soldiers and civilians (an estimate because deaths were not documented by today's standards)

Summary: At that time, the major powers of the world had divided into two camps: the Allies and the Central Powers. In 1914, Germany invaded Belgium. The Allies defended Belgium and the war began. In Europe, much of the war was fought from muddy trenches cut into the countryside. Living and working in these close quarters, the soldiers would stand up and shoot, then duck back down. The trenches were infested with rats. Lice were also a problem. And the bathrooms, called latrines, filled to overflowing.

Fort Riley, Kansas

March 4, 1918

Breakfast

Private Albert Gitchell did not hear the clanging forks against plates as hungry soldiers wolfed down their first meal of the day. Instead, he heard the steady shuffle of nurses' footsteps around his hospital bed. His sore throat ached. His head throbbed with pain. Then chills. He had a fever.

12:00 noon

Illness was spreading through the army base like wildfire. And no wonder! Wartime soldiers were training for battle. They exercised together, marched together, ate together, and slept in beds lined up next to each other in camp-like barracks. By lunchtime, one hundred more soldiers had the same symptoms as Albert. The culprit was influenza, or the flu. But this flu was different from seasonal flu. This flu seemed to be extra-contagious and especially deadly.

DANGER CLUE!

During the coronavirus pandemic that began in 2019, people learned to stay at least six feet (two meters) away from one another. That's because speaking and breathing produce airborne water droplets that can spread disease. This fact was not well understood at the time of the Spanish flu.

United States

Late spring 1918

At military training camps across the country, the nights should have been quiet. After all, soldiers were tired from drills, running, strength training, target practice, and more. But nighttime quiet became a chorus of coughs and groans. Suddenly the flu seemed to be everywhere at once.

DANGER CLUE!

To prepare for battle, 70 million military personnel worldwide were on the move around the globe. That meant their germs were on the move, too. Military personnel spread the disease in training camps and wherever in the world they traveled. The same was true of the people moving support supplies.

And they were not alone. Millions of people all over the world, not just soldiers, became sick with the same symptoms: cough, fever, headache, and, for many, pneumonia. People were dying by the thousands. Hospitals were overrun. Local doctors worked all hours, night and day, trying to help their sick neighbors. The symptoms were more severe, more intense, than any flu they had ever seen. Doctors and nurses ordered patients to rest. Some prescribed herbs. There was little more they could do.

While Albert Gitchell was the first recorded case of this deadly flu, it had quickly spread around the world.

The war made fighting this flu especially difficult. The governments involved in the war wanted to keep morale high. They wanted the soldiers focused on combat, *not* on this mysterious and terrifying new type of flu. And they wanted folks at home to support their efforts by donating money and cheering them on. They needed soldiers to keep training, traveling to the battlefield, and winning.

So the American government and other world leaders downplayed what was happening with the flu. Both the United States and the United Kingdom enacted laws making it hard to report anything that could hurt the war effort. Some newspapers supported this law by censoring news about the severity of the outbreaks or failing to report on them at all.

Spain, on the other hand, was not involved in the war. It was neutral. And so the Spanish government warned Spaniards about the flu. Spanish newspapers ran constant updates. And that's how this flu got its name: Spanish flu. People also called it the Spanish

Lady. The reporting made the flu seem like a problem just for Spain. But that was not the case. By the end of 1918, forty-five thousand American soldiers alone would lose their lives to Spanish flu.

DANGER CLUE!

Getting information to people quickly is critical during a pandemic. That way people can quarantine themselves and take safety steps like wearing masks and washing hands. Keeping news about this deadly virus quiet meant that more people died because they did not know about the danger they were facing.

`Gunnison, Colorado`

`September 27, 1918`

Meanwhile, in the Colorado town of Gunnison, local newspapers were not willing to stay quiet about the flu. The headline of the local paper seemed to echo like thunder through the Rocky Mountain town. One of their boys, who had been training for war, died. Only he didn't die fighting the enemy. No, he died *before* leaving American shores. He was stationed at a fort in New Jersey. And just like that, dead. The article pointed a finger at the killer: Spanish influenza.

Gunnison was a prosperous and growing town. It was known for silver mining and farming, and one of the keys to its prosperity was the railroad. It ran right through town, which meant it was easy to ship goods where they needed to go. The more goods sold, the more money made. But suddenly that railroad seemed like a threat. It was a direct line to the biggest cities of Colorado. If the flu was spreading in those cities, it could surely come to Gunnison.

Specific contagious illnesses are immediately reported to the federal government when they crop up. Today, the flu is on that list. In 1918, it wasn't a reportable illness, so the American government had no accurate way to measure how widespread the disease was or where hot spots were popping up. This made it difficult to quickly understand just how bad the situation was and whether a particular part of the country needed more help than another part.

In Philadelphia, a dazzling parade was planned to boost spirits and raise money for the war effort. This idea horrified many local physicians. Typing away, one doctor spelled it out clearly. The Spanish flu was dangerous, so contagious that people should not gather in crowds, and certainly not attend a parade! The doctor knew what he had to do: send the letter to the newspapers and ask them to publish it. That way, the citizens would be warned. But the papers in Philadelphia refused to publish it. They did not want to hurt the war effort.

Flags lined Broad Street. Two hundred thousand people spilled over the sidewalks along the parade route. The City of Brotherly Love was showing its undying support for American soldiers. Decorated floats drifted past the cheering crowds. Bands marched, playing patriotic songs. The parade not only lifted spirits; it was also raising money. The US government was selling war bonds. When you bought one, you were lending the government money to buy things like supplies and weapons. When the war was over, the government would pay you back with interest. In the meantime, this money would go straight to the war effort and help bring the soldiers back alive. With all the excitement, war bonds sold quickly.

DANGER CLUE!

Paradegoers stood shoulder to shoulder, front to back, in a sea of people. To yell out support, they had to take deep breaths and use a lot of air. Shouting sent droplets of saliva out of people's mouths. These droplets traveled as far as 20 feet (6 meters).

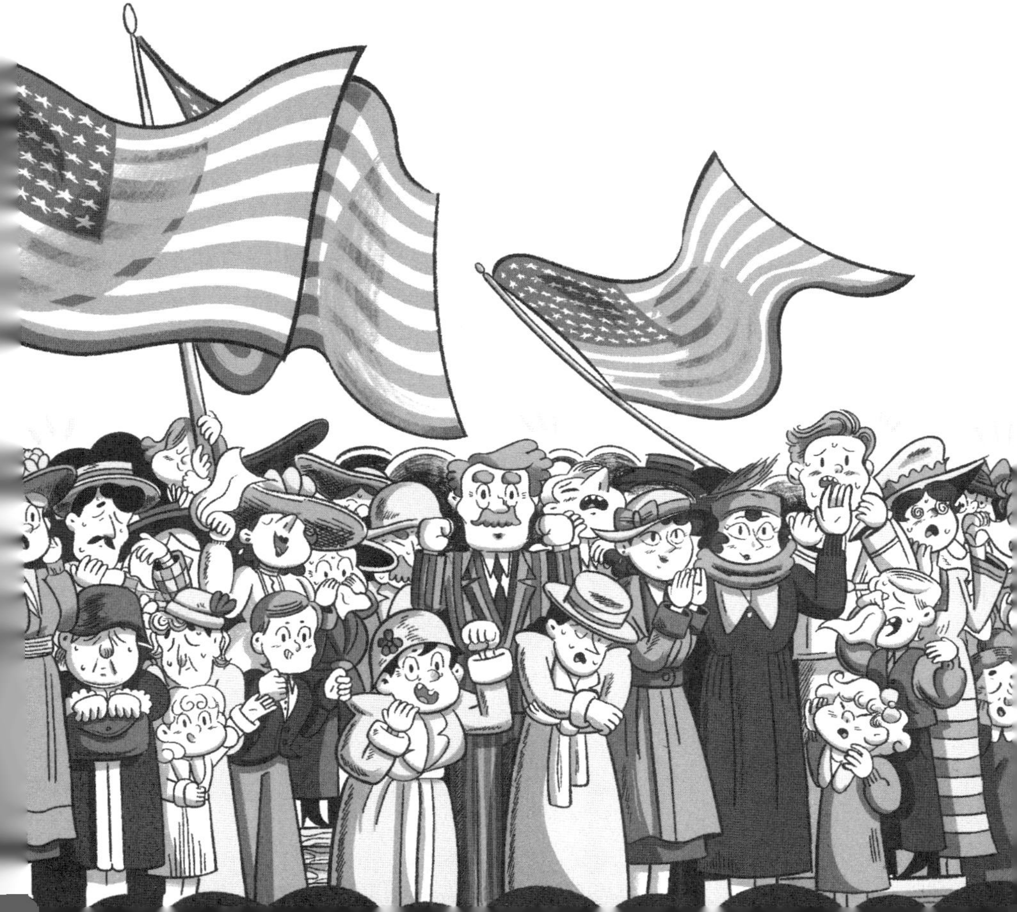

Since people did not take steps to protect themselves from the flu at the parade, the virus spread easily. The number of sick people increased day after day. There wasn't an empty hospital bed to be found. And even though hospitals were filled, the sick kept coming. In just a few weeks, more than twelve thousand people in Philadelphia lost their lives to Spanish flu. The parade had been a superspreader event. Carpenters couldn't build coffins fast enough. Some families had to wait to bury their loved ones. Across the country, the death toll for October alone hit 195,000 people.

Overseas, soldiers were dying of flu by the tens of thousands. Hundreds of thousands were hospitalized. At army camps across the United States, flu outbreaks seemed unending. Some training camps would no longer let the men eat across the table from one another. But because strict efforts to contain the flu were not made and enforced worldwide in the midst of so much troop movement, they did little to stop the virus.

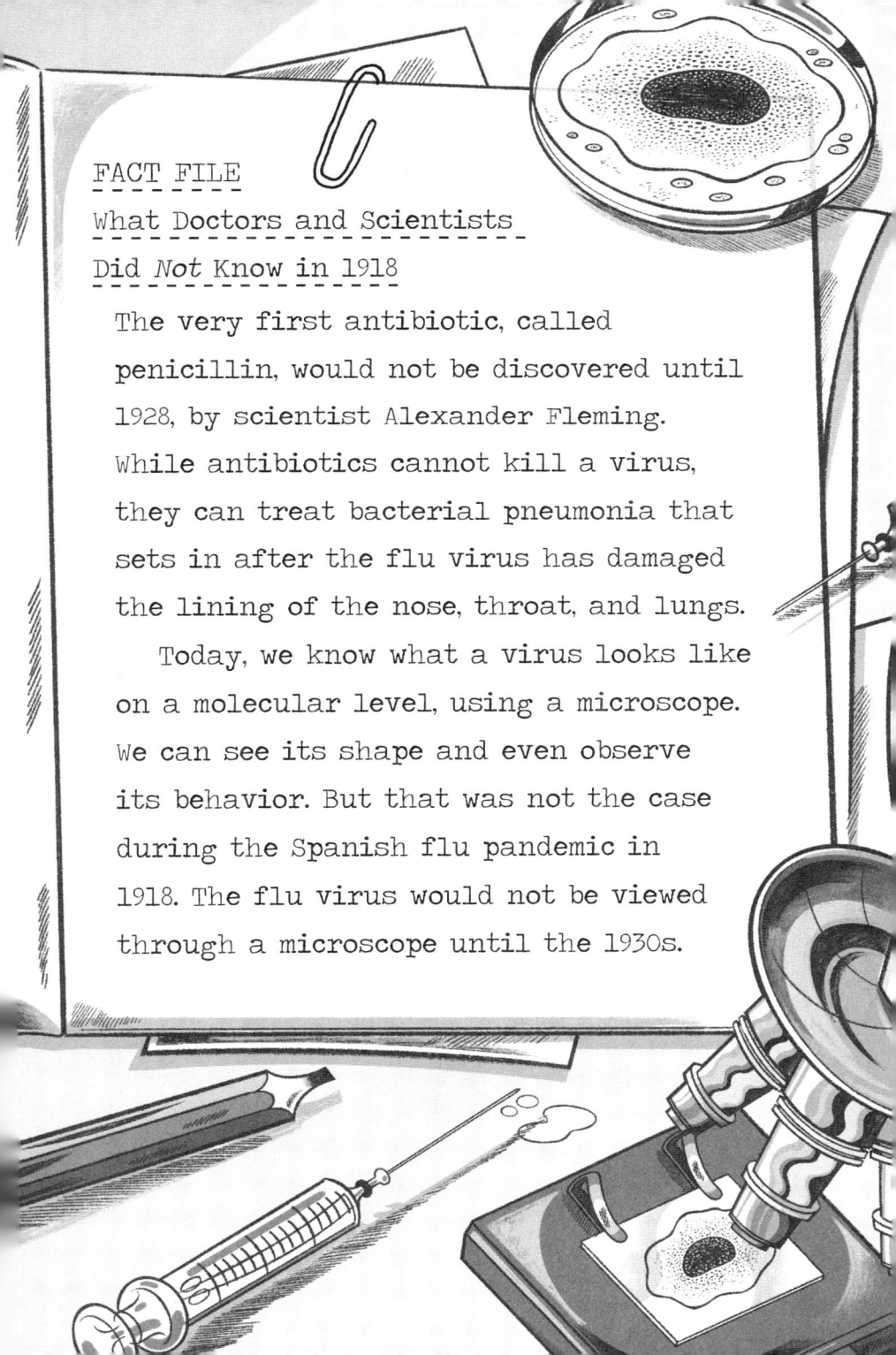

FACT FILE
What Doctors and Scientists
Did *Not* Know in 1918

The very first antibiotic, called
penicillin, would not be discovered until
1928, by scientist Alexander Fleming.
While antibiotics cannot kill a virus,
they can treat bacterial pneumonia that
sets in after the flu virus has damaged
the lining of the nose, throat, and lungs.

Today, we know what a virus looks like
on a molecular level, using a microscope.
We can see its shape and even observe
its behavior. But that was not the case
during the Spanish flu pandemic in
1918. The flu virus would not be viewed
through a microscope until the 1930s.

EYEWITNESS

Name: Edna Register Boone

Born: October 3, 1907

Age: 10

Hometown: Madrid, Alabama

Family: Mother, father, and two brothers

Madrid, Alabama

Edna Boone dropped the bucket down the well, where it hit the water with a splash. Peering down at the bucket, she watched it fill with water. She held the rope tightly with one hand and reached up and wrapped her fingers around the next length of rope. Pulling down with one hand and then the other, Edna hoisted the bucket to the top.

Careful not to spill or slosh, she hauled the water to the house. Mama needed water, and ten-year-old Edna couldn't let her down. Edna heard the sound of the hatchet and caught a glimpse of her twin brothers chopping wood. It was the boys' job to keep the stove and the fireplace going.

She carefully walked into the kitchen and poured the water into the woodstove's reservoir attached to the side of the stove. This water supply was critical in helping her mother.

Mama ladled more water into the pots. In one pot, she boiled water to sanitize glass jars. In another pot, she stirred soup.

Soon, the jars would be filled to the top with nourishing soup and ready to be delivered to sick people. The number of people in town who had fallen ill was growing by the day. They were too sick to work, too sick to go out, and too sick to make meals. Edna and her family were their only hope.

Edna wrapped gauze around her face, covering her mouth and nose just like a mask. Now she was ready to deliver dinner to doorsteps all over town.

Masks work by reducing the number of droplets that leave your mouth and nose and travel into the air in front of you. Gauze is a thin, airy cotton fabric often used for treating wounds. It is not as tightly woven as other types of cotton fabric, so when it was used as a mask during the Spanish flu pandemic, it would not have held back all the droplets coming from the wearer or prevented infection from reaching the person wearing the mask. Some refused to wear masks, even after cities arrested citizens for going mask-free. Some people wore masks outside in public but took them off when socializing with friends in private. Others cut holes in their masks to make it easier to smoke cigarettes.

FACT FILE
World Leaders Who Contracted Spanish Flu
- Prime Minister David Lloyd George, United Kingdom
- Mahatma Gandhi, India
- King Alfonso XIII, Spain

European and American governments may have been able to limit reporters' access to information about how many people got the flu nationwide. But in individual towns and cities, reporters didn't have to rely on the federal government for local information. In small-town America, if someone got sick from Spanish flu, it made the newspaper.

And Gunnison's county doctor was relying on that information to count cases. Scouring the newspaper, talking to state officials, Dr. F. P. Hanson paid close attention to any news of the disease so that he could determine where the flu was spreading. He was not about to let the flu devastate his town, his neighbors.

But what could he do? Dr. Hanson had an idea. He called it "quarantine . . . against the world."

The local board of health gave him the full authority to lay down the law. Dr. Hanson promptly closed the schools. He closed the churches. There would be no parties. No street gatherings. And no one could come in across the county line unless they quarantined for two days. Barricades blocked the main roads into town. Anyone caught breaking the rules would go to jail. Period.

Passengers on trains traveling through Gunnison were warned: If you get off the train even to stretch your legs, you will be escorted to quarantine! Why not let people off the train in Gunnison? They could be carrying the flu, whether they knew it or not. And only one brief interaction could spread the airborne virus to folks in town. The safest thing for everyone was to keep travelers on the trains.

Just two days later, the local newspaper's headline screamed "The 'Flu' Is After Us," with the article warning that "it is circulating in almost every village and community around us."

FACT FILE

Deadly Days

October 1918 was the deadliest month in
America to date; 195,000 Americans died that
month from Spanish flu.

Madrid, Alabama

No one in Edna's family had gotten sick yet. But now, every other family in Madrid had influenza. There were only about two hundred people in town, and almost all of them were sick. Walking home after delivering food, Edna noticed the doctor's office. Wagon after wagon waited for the doctor. Each wagon held a loved one so sick that there was little doubt they would die. Hanging her head, Edna walked the rest of the way home.

Spanish flu was deadly, especially to children under the age of five and people over sixty-five. But it was also deadly to people ages twenty through forty, which made this flu unusual. Sometimes, healthy adults assume they are the least likely to get sick. And often that is true. But Spanish flu was deadly to younger healthy adults. Knowing how deadly a flu is for your age group can help you take better care not to be exposed to the virus.

That night, Edna, her brothers, and her parents prayed. Edna knew she had to keep going. She had to do her part.

Public School No. 17

Indianapolis, Indiana

November 7, 1918

Finally, Beatrice Williams was exactly where she belonged, in her classroom with her friends. There were so many people sick with flu, school had been closed for four whole weeks. Churches were closed, too. Movie theaters were closed. If there was anything fun to do before influenza, it was put on hold. All you could do was stay at home.

FACT FILE

A New Rhyme

Children started skipping rope to a new rhyme:

I had a bird. Her name was Enza.
I opened the window and
In-flew-Enza!

Sitting at her desk, Beatrice paid close attention to Miss Walker. A letter had arrived from Sergeant Armstrong! Miss Walker read it to the class.

And even better? The class assignment was to write him back.

Taking out her pen and a lined sheet of paper, Beatrice began carefully writing. Using her very best cursive, Beatrice told him she'd been sick.

I was a victim of the Influenza, but I am alright now.

The sound of scrawling ink pens filled the room. *It has been a contagious disease here known as the "Spanish Influenza,"* wrote Beatrice's friend Earlee. *Several people have died of it.*

Beatrice and her classmates also wanted Sergeant Armstrong to know that everyone was doing their part to support the troops at war. They raised money. They bought special war stamps. Each class was in competition, trying to raise the most money.

Finally, after filling two pages with news, Beatrice signed her name.

FACT FILE

Devastating Consequences

One example of the flu's path of devastation happened in a small town in Alaska. When traders arrived at Brevig Mission on dogsleds, they were probably carrying the flu with them. Eighty adults lived in the town, but by the end of 1918, only eight adults survived.

In the United States, life expectancy, or how long people are expected to live on average, plummeted in 1918 from fifty-one years old to just thirty-nine.

November 1918

Meanwhile, the war was coming to an end. Finally, on November 11, Germany surrendered. Even though all the details still needed to be worked out and a treaty signed, both sides agreed to put down their weapons. The war was over. Mass celebrations broke out around the world. Church bells rang out. Firehouses blared their alarms. People ran into the streets to cheer.

But the pandemic was not over. With so many people gathered in happiness over the war ending, the virus spread. The effort to bring back millions of troops to their homes began. And as the soldiers traveled home, they brought the flu with them.

The Committee of the American Public Health Association was nervous. They issued a recommendation for people to walk to work instead of taking public transportation. They also asked shop owners to limit how many people could be in their stores at once and asked factories to stagger schedules of workers.

But people at home were exhausted from living in quarantine. The good news of peace made many people want to forget about the flu and live a normal life once again. But that holiday season, the death toll rose again. The church bells rang continuously for funerals.

In San Francisco alone, 1,800 people came down with the flu and more than 100 people died. And that was just in the first week of 1919.

FACT FILE EXPERIMENT
How Do Germs Spread?

1. Sprinkle some powdered chalk onto a counter or into a medium-size bowl. Put your hand palm side down into the chalk. Now shake hands with a friend. Then have that friend shake hands with another person. Keep the chain going for as many people as you have available. What is happening to the chalk?

2. Now repeat the experiment. But this time, after you place your hand in the chalk, wash your hands for sixty seconds with warm soapy water. Then begin the handshake chain. What happened to the chalk this time? What does this tell us about the spread of germs?

Dr. Hanson kept records by reading newspapers from nearby towns and talking to other officials. The number of hospital stays was falling. New cases of flu in communities surrounding Gunnison were low. The same was true for reports of deaths. The worst of it seemed to be over. Two waves of the flu had swept the country. But Gunnison was still safe and now four months into strict quarantine. Dr. Hanson felt like it was at least safe enough for the children of Gunnison to go back to school.

Madrid, Alabama

Edna's heart dropped through her stomach. "Mama!" she called out. "Mama!" Edna could not believe her eyes. Her mother was lying flat out on the floor over by the fireplace. Had the flu finally gotten to their family? Edna started to panic.

"Are you sick?" she called out, terrified.

Her mother stirred. "No, child. I'm just so tired. I wanted to get as close to the fire as I could." After all, Edna's mother had worked day and night to keep the town fed and to take care of her own family. Edna was so relieved that her mom was simply tired. After her nap, Mama was back to work once again. And once again, Edna did everything she could to help.

FACT FILE
Dealing with a Shortage
With so many nurses and doctors overseas, some cities created fast-track nursing programs to quickly train new hires how to care for the sick.

Finally, it seemed safe enough. Dr. Hanson opened the town's borders, opened its churches, allowed parties. Life in Gunnison could finally get back to normal.

The first flu vaccines were not developed until the 1930s. With no vaccine, the world's population had no choice but to do whatever else they could to stem the spread. But without a vaccine, there was no way to stop the virus completely. If there had been a vaccine, fewer people would have died.

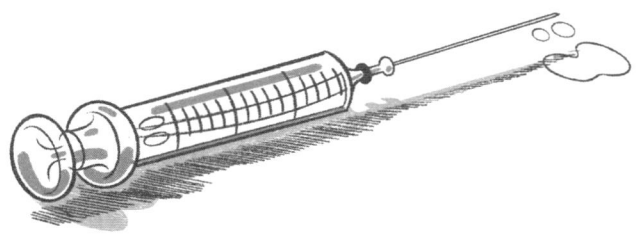

Madrid, Alabama

Edna watched as her father and brothers worked in the yard along the side of the house. It was a quarter of an acre. They carefully turned over the soil. No one in town had been able to farm, shop, or even cook. The residents were in need of food. Soon Edna's family would plant sweet potatoes, enough to feed themselves and the community.

Gunnison, Colorado
March 1919

Grabbing his medical bag, Dr. Hanson rushed out. All of a sudden, people were getting sick. Cough. Fever. Headache. Dr. Hanson didn't have any doubt. Despite his best efforts to keep his community safe, the flu had finally made it to Gunnison. One hundred people came down with it. And five died from pneumonia. Even so, the third wave was not nearly as deadly as the first two. And because Dr. Hanson had insisted that Gunnison cut itself off from the world for a time, a lot of lives were saved.

FACT FILE
Open-Air Hospitals

In Boston, Massachusetts, emergency hospitals were set up outside in the fresh air and sunlight. Today, researchers believe that those open-air hospitals saved many lives because the virus had a more difficult time spreading when exposed to the sun and fresh air. Those Boston hospital workers also used face masks and washed their hands.

English nurse Florence Nightingale had written years earlier about how helpful fresh air was in tending the sick. Unfortunately, her idea had not become standard practice. Some doctors began keeping track of death rates at regular hospitals versus outdoor hospitals. Inside, the death rate was about 40 percent. Outside, it was down to 13 percent.

Doctors and nurses around the country looked at something they had not seen in a while: empty hospital beds. Fewer people were catching the flu. Fewer people were dying. And by fall, it was over. The Spanish flu's terrible run came to a stop.

FACT FILE

Deadly Tally

By June 1919, more than five hundred thousand Americans had died from the Spanish flu.

The war was over. The flu was gone. Irven Armstrong stood once again at the chalkboard full of math problems, giving his all to his students and demanding the very best of them. The treasured letters he had received from his students during the war were safely stored at home.

As the hustle and bustle of life resumed, Edna noticed that some things had changed. Families were closer than ever, having spent so much time quarantined together. Even her little town was closer. They had grieved together, and they had helped one another. And those memories would stay with them for the rest of their lives. The flu was gone, and a big harvest of potatoes planted during the pandemic would bring the community together one more time.

A note about our eyewitness Edna. You'll notice this chapter largely follows a location-and-time format. When Edna gave interviews about her experience of Spanish flu, she did not offer specific dates. However, she did give a lot of clues as to when these events happened over the two-year pandemic. Using Edna's information and news reports of how the virus spread in her area, events are placed in this narrative to the best of our ability for accuracy.

FACT FILE

The Spanish Flu

Scientific name: H1N1

Origin: Avian (from birds). No one is sure exactly which country Spanish flu came from, though the first reported case was in the United States.

Symptoms: Fatigue, sore throat, fever, chills, cough, and often severe pneumonia, which was deadly

Number of people infected: Approximately 500 million people around the globe, about one-third of the world's population

Number of people who died: Approximately 50 million. Some experts think that the number may actually be as high as 100 million.

IMPACT ⚡

Historical Record

Irven Armstrong died in 1996 at 104 years old. The letters from his students were discovered, safely tucked away, as part of his estate.

Forget and Repeat?

Once the pandemic (and World War I) ended, people quickly moved on, trying not to talk about that terrible time. It felt good to not be constantly worried about getting the flu, dying, or losing loved ones! The Spanish flu and its devastation was added to history books and left out of daily conversation.

That said, today, modern scientists and researchers continue to investigate past outbreaks like the Spanish flu pandemic to understand if they could happen again. The answer is yes. Many scientists have been warning various government leaders for years. Researchers even came up with pandemic preparedness plans. Still, their work was not prioritized or well funded as the world focused on other problems. Ultimately, their warnings were not taken seriously enough to prevent another devastating pandemic.

COVID-19

When the COVID-19 pandemic spread around the globe in 2020, many people turned to stories from the time of Spanish flu to learn from that pandemic. But the world had a vital tool this time: the quick development of vaccines.

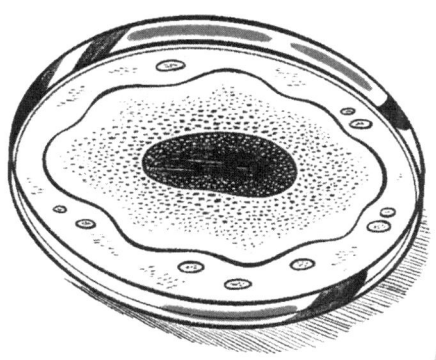

Chapter 4
THE BOSTON MOLASSES FLOOD

EYEWITNESS

Name: Antonio DiStasio

Age: 9

Hometown: Boston, Massachusetts

Family: Mother, Carmela; father, Vincenzo;
and sister, Maria

Nine-year-old Antonio DiStasio woke up with a throbbing headache and that panicked feeling of not knowing where he was. Why was he under a sheet? Antonio took a deep breath. Wait! Where was his sister, Maria?

Antonio tore the sheet off his face. Shocked nurses rushed to his side. They couldn't believe it. Emergency workers had covered his body with a sheet because they thought he was dead. But Antonio was very much alive!

Antonio realized he was in some kind of hospital. But something about the place was different. It was the nurses' uniforms. They should have been white and clean. Instead, they were covered in sticky brown streaks and smudges. The sweet smell of molasses filled Antonio's nose. *Molasses? The explosion! What happened?*

FACT FILE
Molasses

Molasses is a thick, syrupy liquid made from sugarcane, a plant grown in the Caribbean islands. Steamer ships from Cuba, the West Indies, and Puerto Rico brought large quantities into Boston Harbor, where it was stored in a giant tank near the wharfs. Some of this molasses was distilled into alcohol, to be used in making rum. Most of it was distilled into industrial alcohol, an ingredient used in making dynamite and other munitions.

THREE DAYS EARLIER . . .

Boston, Massachusetts

North End Neighborhood: Commercial Street

January 12, 1919

11:00 a.m.

FACT FILE

Locale

The North End is a Boston neighborhood. In 1919, this harborside area was home to many Italian immigrants.

Water sloshed against the metal hull of the ship *Miliero* as it cruised into Boston Harbor. Braving freezing temperatures, workers gathered on the wharf to dock the ship and unload its cargo.

They had their work cut out for them. After they tied up the ship, they connected the discharge hoses to both the ship and the permanent pipeline at the wharf. The hydraulic pumps whirred to life to move

600,000 gallons (two million liters) of sweet goopy molasses out of the ship and into the towering storage tank rising over Boston's North End neighborhood.

FACT FILE

The Molasses Tank

Location: Commercial Street, between the harbor and the railroad tracks

Owner: US Industrial Alcohol

Height: 50 feet (15 meters)

Circumference: 240 feet (73 meters)

Construction: A cylinder made of eighteen steel plates; seams fastened in place with rivets; topped by a steel domed cap

Capacity: 2.3 million gallons (8.7 million liters). That means it would take water from THREE Olympic-size swimming pools to fill this tank.

Weight of a tankful of molasses: 13,000 tons (12,000 metric tons; almost as much as the Brooklyn Bridge)

DANGER CLUE!

The land for the tank was leased in September 1915, and its construction had been rushed. The tank was first filled with molasses just two days after the construction was completed, at the end of December 1915. Under pressure from the tank owners, builders skipped an important step. They did not test the finished tank. To do so, they would have filled it with water and inspected it for leaks and any other problems.

Hours of hard work passed. The tank already had molasses in it, and that molasses was cold. After all, it had been shipped to Boston two weeks ago. But this new shipment was still warm. It came from a warm part of the world, traveling quickly in the warmer waters of the Gulf Stream. This molasses had not fully cooled, a process that would take several days in Boston's freezing temperatures.

When cold molasses and warm molasses are mixed, it sparks fermentation. That process releases carbon dioxide, a gas. Since the carbon dioxide had no way to escape, it created pressure on the steel tank.

Co2

Co2

Co2

Co2

Co2

Co2

HOT MOLASSES

Co2

Co2

Co2

Co2

Co2

COLD MOLASSES

127

As the tank filled, the workers noticed loud, strange noises as the two shipments of molasses mixed inside the tank. Even the metal walls seemed to be vibrating. Foam burbled to the top of the molasses tank.

DANGER CLUE!

The captain of the *Miliero* noticed that the molasses tank leaked. It made him sick to his stomach because this tank's seams leaked more than any tank he had ever seen. In fact, the first leak in Boston's tank had been spotted along a single seam several months after the tank was built. Over time, every seam leaked, even when they were caulked. So the tank's structure itself was a problem. And now these weak seams were under pressure from the fermentation caused by mixing cold and warm molasses.

The company that owned the tank was allowed to build it in one of Boston's most populated neighborhoods. It was bustling with workers coming and going, markets, and children playing. And one of the places where children loved playing most was near the molasses tank.

Anti-Italian bigotry was very strong in Boston and the rest of the United States during this time. Italians were discriminated against and sometimes physically attacked. Many immigrant families during this time were focused on getting work to feed their families. These newest Americans did not have political power. And when a powerful company built a molasses tank in their crowded neighborhood, they had no ability to fight it.

With any industrial tank, there is always some risk of failure. There is always some safety concern. The people of the North End did not have the power to make their worries about the tank known. It is still often the case that dangerous industrial buildings and structures are built in or near the poorest communities, putting people at risk.

The North End was home to Italian immigrants just finding their way in America. The houses were built very close together. Building inspections to make sure these homes were safe were careless and lax. Population density is the number of people living in a defined area, and in the North End of Boston, the population density was very high. This increased the likelihood that more people would be endangered if there was a problem.

A handful of neighborhood kids were on a mission: to collect sticks for firewood for their families. It felt like a spring day in Boston—a snow-free, not-too-cold day in the middle of winter. It was a relief after the previous weekend's bone-chilling weather. Even so, cold temperatures were sure to come roaring back, and the kindling would help keep their families warm. There were always sticks near the railroad tracks by the big molasses tank.

Nine-year-old Antonio hid behind the mammoth molasses tank that towered above the train yard. It was just across the street from the apartment building where Antonio lived with his mom, dad, and eleven-year-old sister, Maria. And right now, Maria was in quite a bit of trouble.

Oh no! This wasn't good at all!

Antonio and his friends carefully peered around the tank, watching as rail workers gave Maria quite a lecture. After all, it was a dangerous place to play. The workers yelled at Maria. They wanted Maria to leave.

DANGER CLUE!

In just a day, the weather went from 2°F (-17°C) to 40°F (4°C). Warmer temperatures meant more fermentation within the tank and even more pressure on its already weak and leaking seams. This was a recipe for disaster.

The trick to gathering wood was not getting caught by railroad employees as Maria had. Even better? If you could do the job, not get caught, *and* take a stealthy swipe of that syrupy sweet liquid leaking from the molasses tank. Sometimes so much molasses leaked from the seams and rivets, you could use a stick to scrape molasses off the tank and let it ooze into your bucket until you filled it to the top—and take that home as well!

But now Maria was in trouble. Busted! Antonio had a decision to make: keep hiding or go help his sister.

People who worked near the molasses tank reported feeling the tank vibrate. One witness said it was almost as if the tank was "bulging in and out." As fermentation increased and produced more gas, pressure on the tank increased. As the pressure increased, so did the movement of the molecules that made up the molasses. That pressure exerted force on the sides of the tank, causing vibration. The constant bubbling of gas inside the tank only added to the vibration.

When you attend a ball game and sit on a metal bleacher, you feel it when someone at the other end of the row accidentally kicks the bleacher; the vibration travels through the metal. Similarly, all the vibration in the molasses tank traveled through the metal. If you had put your hand on the tank, you could have felt it. When pressure increases, at some point, that will stress a container until it fails.

12:45 p.m.

A loud rumble came from the tank. Antonio heard Maria scream. He looked up. The tank burst open, letting loose a huge wave of molasses that was headed right for him. Antonio ran away as fast as he could.

DANGER CLUE!

The wave of molasses was 25 feet (8 meters) high (taller than a two-story building!) and 165 feet (50 meters) across (roughly half the length of a football field). It weighed 26 million pounds (11.8 million kilograms). And it was traveling fast: 35 miles (56 kilometers) per hour! Think about that wave's weight and volume—that wall of molasses was unstoppable until it ran its course.

The sound of tearing metal caught the attention of a rail worker. He watched the molasses tank split and saw the heavy brown wave. He witnessed the wave ripping apart a metal support that held up elevated train tracks. And now he saw an oncoming train headed down those tracks to disaster! He had to get the engineer's attention or the train would plunge to the syrupy street below. Racing against time, the worker sounded the emergency alarm. Just in the nick of time, the engineer pulled the brake and stopped the locomotive.

The dark-brown wave caught up to Antonio in an instant and knocked him off his feet. He was trapped in the fast-moving thick liquid. Antonio panicked. Like a bulldozer, the molasses mowed down everything in its path and carried it away in pieces.

One section of the molasses tank was now moving at 35 miles (56 kilometers) per hour with the molasses. It slammed into the local firehouse, pushing it off its foundation and down the street.

Unlike a tsunami coming ashore in one direction, this wave moved in all directions out from the tank. That meant that nothing around it was safe.

The deadly brown wave was full of bricks, big pieces of metal, entire buildings, wagons, pipes, and drowning horses. It tossed Antonio in one direction and then another. Antonio could not control his body. He could not escape. Pain exploded in his mouth as the molasses hurled him face-first into a street curb, knocking out two teeth. Then a piece of metal clonked Antonio on the head. He was cut and bleeding.

In the middle of the churning chaos, Antonio heard someone screaming his name. It was his mother! But her voice grew faint as the wave carried him out toward the harbor. If he could just shout back. But molasses filled his mouth and then his throat. He couldn't call out. And now it was hard to breathe.

A firefighter saw Antonio. He grabbed a long pole and held it out, hoping the boy could grasp it. Antonio started to choke. Desperate, he reached out for the end of the pole. This was his only chance to survive. His sticky fingers closed around the metal. And he held on.

Fighting against the thick molasses, the firefighter strained and struggled. Reaching with one hand and then the other, he pulled the pole toward him. The firefighter had to keep his grip or the boy would be lost. With one final pull, Antonio was close enough to grab. Antonio was safe! But his world turned blurry. The molasses still made it difficult to breathe. And the gash on his head was oozing blood. Antonio passed out.

12:47 p.m.

The violent wave dragged people into the harbor. The water was freezing cold. And it was now filled with bales of hay, rope, pieces of houses, wheels, barrels, animals, and other debris. Some of it floated on the surface; some of it lurked just beneath, where it could catch on the legs of the people struggling for their lives.

One of the workers at the molasses tank had sent multiple warnings to the company. He had warned about the noises, the foam, the leaks, and the vibration. He wondered if the gas buildup would cause the tank to explode. His bosses were no help. The company only added new paint to the tank or made quick fixes that did not address the cause of the problems.

12:50 p.m.

Just as quickly as the 25-foot (7.6-meter) wave of heavy molasses escaped its giant tank, destroying almost everything in its path . . . it dwindled, dropping down, down, down until the only thing left of that gigantic wave was a sticky goo-covered mess.

Only five minutes had gone by, but five minutes was all it took for Antonio's North End neighborhood to become a complete disaster.

A sticky brown trail crept its way throughout Boston, along sidewalks, into trains, streetcars,

apartment buildings, businesses, and houses. It was tracked across the city by people who came and went from the disaster scene. Wherever feet went, so did molasses. Some buildings were now nothing more than a pile of splintered sticks and bricks. Others had been moved in one piece or were left with only one room standing.

People were missing. Some were trapped. Some had drowned. Some had been dragged out into the harbor by the molasses wave. Wounded survivors cried out for help.

Emergency workers from all over Boston and even sailors in the harbor rushed to the scene. They found chaos and devastation. Rescuers used blow-torches to cut through metal debris to free trapped victims. Soon they also had brown molasses on their feet, legs, hands, clothes, and even in their hair.

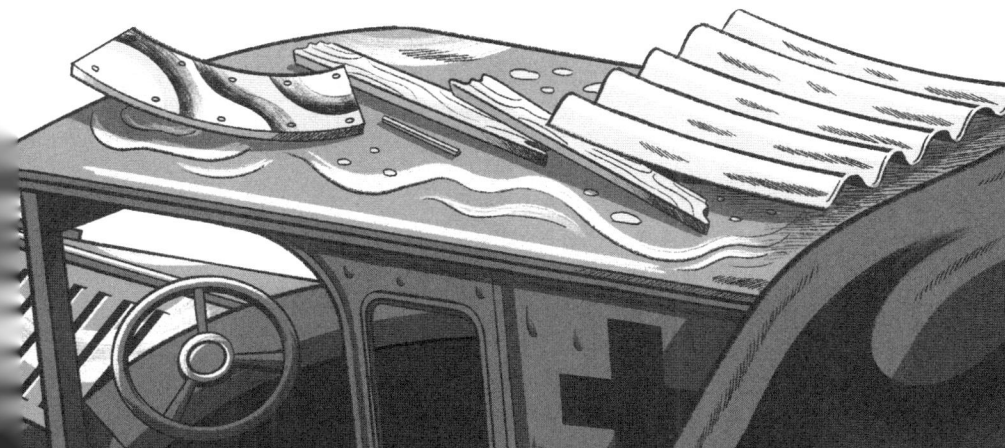

FACT FILE

Women Heroes

World War I had just ended and many men
were still overseas. When the Red Cross
arrived with a caravan of ambulances,
women were in charge.

Stunned and upset, people looked for missing friends and family members. They also searched for their belongings—furniture, money, clothes, horses, wagons, and food.

Antonio's parents frantically searched through pools of hardening molasses. Where was Antonio? Where was Maria? The molasses wave had traveled in all directions. They could be anywhere. Minutes quickly turned to hours as their search dragged on.

By the end of the afternoon, Antonio's parents finally had good news. Antonio was alive! He had a terrible fracture to his skull, but he was alive. But what about their daughter, Maria? There was still no word. They had to keep looking.

Thursday, January 16, 1919

READ ALL ABOUT IT!

HUGE MOLASSES TANK EXPLODES!

The headlines showed the horror. The neighborhood was unrecognizable in the news photos. Only through captions could you know what you were looking at.

While Bostonians read the papers, Antonio and his parents received terrible news of their own. Maria had died in the flood. And so had their young friend Pasquale.

FACT FILE
Sticky Measurement

Imagine dropping a metal ball into a tall glass of water. The ball would fall quickly to the bottom. But if you drop that same ball into a glass of honey, it would take longer for the ball to reach the bottom because honey is thicker, or more viscous, than water. The measurement of that thickness is called viscosity. Molasses is more than five thousand times more viscous than water.

Friday, January 17, 1919

News of the disaster traveled around the world. People learned just how dangerous a molasses wave could be. Back in Boston, the mayor and citizens wanted answers. What had caused the tank to fall apart? Who was to blame?

There was only one way to find out: investigate. Inspectors and investigators swarmed the disaster scene, searching for clues. While they gathered evidence and data, families like Antonio's were left to pick up the pieces. Not only were lives lost, personal belongings ruined, and buildings destroyed, but they also had to clean molasses off of just about everything. Firefighters even pumped salt water from the harbor to help rid the North End of the goopy mess.

Eventually the investigation wrapped up and it was time to explain in court everything that had been uncovered. Antonio was one of many eyewitnesses who testified. Once the trial was over, the judge came to one conclusion: the owner of the storage tank was to blame. And major changes would have to be made to keep something like this from ever happening again.

FACT FILE
Tragedy by the Numbers
  Dead:
  · 20 horses
  · 19 adults
  · 2 kids (Maria and her friend
    Pasquale Iantosca)
  Injured:
  · 150 people

As for Antonio, he lived a long life—he became a boxer, fell in love, and got married. But he would never forget that deadly day. And neither would anyone else who lived in that neighborhood. For decades after the explosion, on the very hottest days, you could still catch a whiff of the sweet molasses that had seeped into and been absorbed by soil, basements, masonry, and wood.

FACT FILE EXPERIMENT

How Do You Clean an Ooey-Gooey Mess?

Cover two small plates with warm molasses. Let the molasses cool. Now try to clean them using cold tap water on one surface and cold salt water on the other. Which works best? Why do you think that is? How could your results have helped people clean up after the molasses disaster?

IMPACT!

Investigation

In April 1925, after six years of investigation and hearings, the judge (actually an auditor, or court-appointed legal expert) on the case blamed the owners of the tank. He said the tank had been built too fast and hadn't been properly tested. And the company did not take enough action when they found out that the tank was leaking.

Additionally, the judge pointed out the danger in building a tank like that so close to a crowded neighborhood. He awarded the victims $300,000. Today, that would be worth $4.4 million. But some felt they deserved more. So the company reached an agreement to pay twice as much to the victims—which in today's money is close to $10 million. After the award, another difficult task began. The legal team had to figure out how much to give to each injured survivor and how much to give to families who'd lost loved ones.

Suspicions

There had been unrest in Boston at the time of the molasses flood. Some thought a group of people called anarchists were to blame. Anarchists believe that people will have better lives without a government in charge. Sometimes, to make their point, they became violent. After the molasses tank exploded, people wondered if anarchists had planted a bomb in the tank. The investigation did not uncover any evidence of a bomb.

Change

How did this terrible tragedy change things for the better? Bostonians agreed to pay higher taxes (or give the government more money) so that inspectors could take a close look at plans for new buildings, the construction process, and the finished structure. These inspections would help with safety, quality, crowding, and how close new structures were built to other buildings and to residential neighborhoods.

Today

You can visit the Commercial Street site of the molasses tank in Boston's North End neighborhood. The site is now a park with a safe place for kids to play.

Chapter 5
THE *HINDENBURG*

EYEWITNESS

Name: Werner Franz

Born: May 22, 1922

Age: 14

Hometown: Frankfurt-Bonames, Germany

Family: Mother, father, and brother

Employer: Deutsche Zeppelin-Reederei

Job: Cabin boy

Fourteen-year-old Werner Franz could not believe his luck. He had been looking for an apprenticeship for months. His father was out of work, and Werner needed a job to help support the family. His mother was counting on him, and he did not want to let her down. All those months, and still no job. But now everything had changed—all because of a chance meeting.

Werner had just landed a job working on one of the most amazing airships in the world, the *Hindenburg*. His brother worked at a hotel in Frankfurt, where the airship's captain and crew happened to be staying. Werner's brother had heard the captain say he needed to hire a cabin boy to take care of the ship's officers. And now? Werner had the job! Not only could he earn money for his family, but this was also his chance to see the world. Not to mention the fact that of all the airships ever made, the *Hindenburg*'s luxury could not be beat. What an opportunity!

FACT FILE

The *Hindenburg*

Airship type: This dirigible (or airship)
was lighter than air because it was filled
with hydrogen gas. The captain controlled
his airship's speed and direction of travel.
Water was placed in the bottom of the
ship before it took off to make it heavier,
keeping it on the ground. When it was ready
to rise, the water was dumped. To land,
hydrogen was released to make the airship
less buoyant.

Captain: Max Pruss

Construction cost: $3 million

Construction details: Metal frame of
aluminum alloy. Gas cells made with two
layers of coated cotton. Four 16-cylinder
engines, each providing 1,320 horsepower at
top speed. Massive tail rudder for steering.
Passenger quarters in two-story gondola.
Control car where captain piloted the ship
located toward front of ship's underbelly.

<u>Owner</u>: Deutsche Zeppelin-Reederei

<u>Investor</u>: German government, controlled by Nazi Party. Nazi money helped pay for the development and construction of the *Hindenburg*. The *Hindenburg* was decorated with the Nazi symbol, the swastika, and the Nazi Party used the airship as propaganda. That means they used the fantastic spectacle of this airship to make the Nazis look good.

<u>Measurements</u>:

- 804 feet (245 meters) long (almost as long as the *Titanic*)
- 134 feet (41 meters) wide

<u>Speed</u>: 80 miles (130 kilometers) per hour

<u>First flight</u>: March 4, 1936

DANGER CLUE!

The hydrogen that enabled the airship to fly was held in cells like pillows inside the *Hindenburg*. This kept the hydrogen from mixing with air. When hydrogen is mixed with air, it's very dangerous. A single spark can cause a powerful explosion.

May 6, 1937

4:10 p.m.

Werner was excited. It had taken only three days to travel from his home in Germany all the way across the Atlantic Ocean. Three days! An ocean liner took at least a couple of weeks. But the airship? It passed ocean liners down below as it sailed over the ocean! Werner had already made *three* round trips across the Atlantic aboard the *Hindenburg*. He had already seen parts of South America and North America. But traveling never got old. On one trip to Rio de Janeiro, there was a three-day layover and Werner got to go horseback riding and he had a chance to hang out at the beach. Each trip brought new adventure.

When passengers lined up to board the Hindenburg, they opened their bags for inspection. Crew members made sure luggage did not contain any matches, pipes, lighters, or flashbulbs that attached to cameras—nothing that could create a spark, because the Hindenburg was so flammable. If they found any of these items, they took them away and stored them during the flight. Once the airship landed, passengers could claim these belongings.

Werner's job as a cabin boy meant attending to the officers' needs. He helped with clearing their dinner plates, making beds, shining shoes, washing dishes, and whatever else needed to be done. If there was any down time on the voyages, he loved hanging out with the crew, laughing and sometimes playing music. Occasionally, Werner glimpsed famous people on board. The cost of a one-way ticket to the United States was $400, as much as a car! Werner loved everything about his assignment and dreamed of becoming a captain one day.

FACT FILE

The Lap of Luxury

The *Hindenburg* offered its passengers, some of whom were celebrities, delicious meals, comfortable heated cabins, and beautiful common areas, including a wall of windows for taking in the view. The dining room's walls were covered in sumptuous silk fabric.

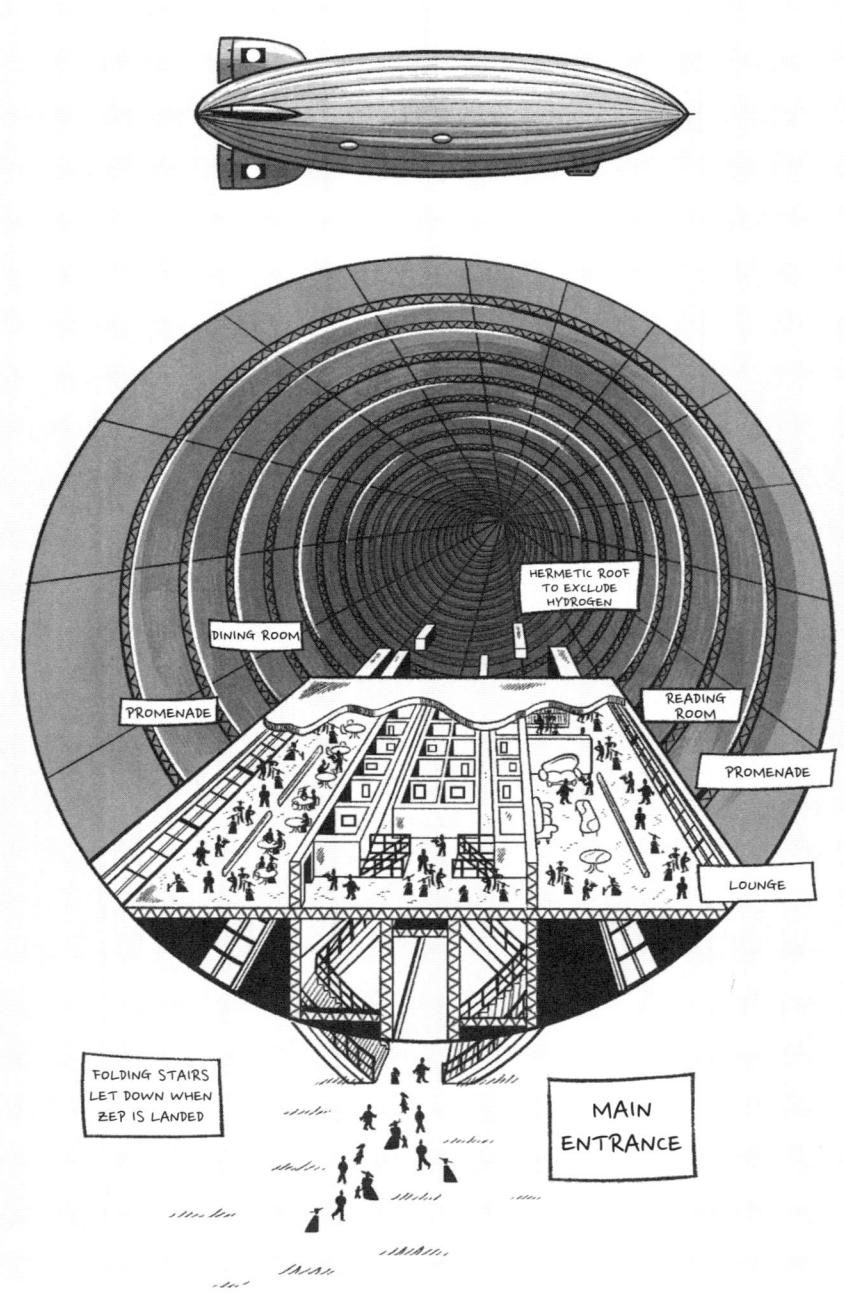

HINDENBURG CROSS SECTION

Looking at the pocket watch his grandfather had given him, Werner knew they should have been landing in Lakehurst, New Jersey, but the weather there wasn't good enough. Too many storms in the area. They would need to keep their distance until the storms passed. That meant less time on the ground for day trips or dinner out. But on the plus side, Captain Pruss had to kill time to allow the weather to clear. And he did that by treating everyone on board to an aerial tour of Boston and New York City. To Werner, Manhattan looked like a sea of buildings and the people down below looked like ants in an anthill. What a sight!

DANGER CLUE!

Thunderstorms mean the atmosphere is full of positive electrical charge at the top of the clouds and negative electrical charge at the bottom of the clouds. The ground below also has a positive charge. Because opposites attract, the charges create lightning. Even after a thunderstorm, there can be enough electrical charge left in the atmosphere to create sparks.

7:20 p.m.

Walking through the mess hall, where the crew ate, Werner placed dirty silverware on the plate. Picking up one plate and then another, he had to quickly clear the crew's dinner table. It was time for the *Hindenburg* to land. Hovering, the ship was completely still. Werner kept working. Next on his to-do list: putting the clean coffee cups away in the cupboard.

DANGER CLUE!

The floating ship was nearly motionless as it waited to land. But two witnesses on the ground spotted a flutter that could not have come from the ship's slight movements. The witnesses said it looked like gas was escaping from some loose fabric just beside the rear port, or left, engine.

Lakehurst, New Jersey

May 6, 1937

7:20 p.m.

EYEWITNESS

Name: Herb Morrison

Born: May 14, 1905

Age: 31

Hometown: Connellsville, Pennsylvania

Employer: WLS, a radio station in Chicago

Job: News reporter

It wouldn't be much longer now. The *Hindenburg*, a giant lighter-than-air ship, would be landing right in front of Herb Morrison. As a news reporter, Herb had already covered many stories, but this one was especially exciting. Airships like the *Hindenburg* had become the fastest way to travel across the Atlantic Ocean. The ship had ninety-seven people on board. Herb couldn't wait to ask them about their trip.

The *Hindenburg* was filled with seven million cubic feet (200,000 cubic meters) of a gas called hydrogen. Hydrogen is extremely flammable. A cubic foot is a measurement of volume. So imagine a box that is one foot wide, one foot deep, and one foot high. Imagine you fill that cube with something like gas or water or candy. Now you have one cubic foot of something.

Herb was using some new technology for the first time—a Presto Direct Disc recorder. This device would allow him to record his story live, to be played back later to the American public. Herb would narrate the landing event as it happened, and his sound engineer would record it onto a lacquer-coated aluminum disc. As Herb spoke, a needle would drag across the disc, making grooves. The record would later be played on a special machine called a record player that read those grooves and translated them back into sound. The new equipment was heavy and hard to maneuver, but this was the perfect time to test it. And Herb personally loved all things aviation. He couldn't wait to share his report with listeners.

DANGER CLUE!

The Hindenburg was originally designed to use helium instead of hydrogen. Helium, unlike hydrogen, is not flammable. So why was the Hindenburg using flammable hydrogen? Because the largest supply of helium came from the United States. And the US government did not allow helium to be sold to any other country, for fear it could be used in war.

7:25 p.m.

With the record spinning on the new equipment, Herb's sound engineer pulled his headphones over his ears. All Herb had to do was start talking about what he was seeing.

The Hindenburg was the largest airship built. Its width made it more stable than previous airships. And its overall size meant it could carry more hydrogen gas.

When the *Hindenburg* was in sight, Herb Morrison looked out over the vast airfield. Then he moved in close to the microphone and began to describe the *Hindenburg*'s approach.

"Well, here it comes, ladies and gentlemen; we're out now, outside of the hangar," he said in a smooth voice. "And what a great sight it is, a thrilling one, just a marvelous sight. It's coming down out of the sky." His enthusiasm for air travel came right through the microphone.

The airship's silver coating wasn't just for show. Called dope, the silver paint made the *Hindenburg*'s cotton cover waterproof. When builders laced the covering around the frame, the dope was applied. As the dope dried, it shrank the covering tightly around the ship's rigid aluminum-alloy skeleton. Dope was made of aluminum powder and a type of varnish, both of which were flammable. In modern times, aluminum powder and the same varnish-like ingredient are used to make a type of rocket fuel.

As Herb spoke, he didn't miss a detail: the shiny exterior, the polish on the propellers, the observation deck. He reported the work of the ground crew as they prepared to help the *Hindenburg* land. He even imagined what the passengers must be doing: "Probably lining the windows looking down at the field ahead of them."

The *Hindenburg* stopped. It hovered quietly above the landing site. Ropes dropped from the airship to tie it to the ground.

And then—the unthinkable.

"It burst into flames!" Herb shouted as the *Hindenburg* exploded before his eyes.

Panic filling his voice, Herb cried out, "It is burning, bursting into flames and is falling. . . . Oh, the humanity and all the passengers!"

One of those passengers was Werner Franz. As Herb recorded the horror, Werner was inside the fireball, fighting for his life.

DANGER CLUE!

The large volume of hydrogen meant there was a lot of gas to fuel the fire. A bigger fire burns hotter, and the sheer size of the fire made surviving it very difficult.

What was that? Werner heard a thud. He steadied himself as the ship shook. It felt as if the floor was coming out from under him. The ship suddenly lurched, tilting up. With a roar, flames exploded above him.

Only a burnt-out frame and ashes would be left of the ship in thirty-two seconds. To survive, Werner would have to get out, and fast.

The fire broke open a water tank. Suddenly a deluge of water poured down on Werner. He was drenched from head to toe, his clothes soaked all the way through. The heat was intense. Just then, Werner spotted a hatch. It had been used to load food into the great ship. Desperate to escape, Werner used all of his strength to kick the hatch open with both feet. The *Hindenburg* was falling fast. Werner watched the ground. As soon as it was close enough, he could jump.

Just as passengers' lighters and flashbulbs were a threat to the Hindenburg's safety, so was a positive electrical charge in the atmosphere. Explosions need key ingredients to happen: fuel (like hydrogen), oxygen (part of the Earth's atmosphere), and a spark. The hydrogen provided fuel; the airship was loaded with it, and the flutter of the Hindenburg's outer cover tells us that it was leaking. There was oxygen in the atmosphere. And the positive electrical charges created a spark. An explosion was almost inevitable.

Werner waited. Just one more second. Then he . . . jumped! As soon as he hit the ground, Werner leaped to his feet. Would the flaming inferno fall on top of him? Just then, the bow of the ship rose up. Now Werner could escape! He stretched one foot in front of the other as fast as he could to run away from the flaming wreckage.

How close passengers and crew were to an exit or opening had a major impact on whether they could escape this disaster. Passengers who were sitting closer to a window or opening to the outside could escape more quickly than those who were closer to the interior of the ship.

He was safe. Only thirty-two seconds had passed since the first thud. And now there was nothing left of the *Hindenburg* but a burnt-out frame.

FACT FILE EXPERIMENT
Zap! Can Friction Create a Spark?

Blow up a balloon and tie off the end. Rub the balloon back and forth on a wool hat or wool sweater for a couple of minutes. Next, hold the balloon close to a compact fluorescent light bulb. What happens? Can you guess why?

HINT: This works best in a darkened room.

Herb Morrison watched the whole disaster. He was trying to make sense of it when he broke down. Still recording, he said, "This is the worst of the worst catastrophes in the world. . . . I can't talk, ladies and gentlemen. . . . I—I can hardly breathe. I—I'm gonna step inside where I cannot see it. . . . This is the worst thing I've ever witnessed."

Clothing mattered. One ground crew worker was wearing the wool sweater his grandmother had knitted for him, and it had just been soaked through by earlier rainstorms. He survived uninjured. Some materials catch fire more easily than others. Wool, especially wet wool, is naturally fire resistant, and today many firefighters use it as a base layer when they are on the job and suit up.

Herb took a minute to breathe, to try to face what was happening and do his job—collect as much information as possible. But it wasn't easy. The passengers who had survived were in shock. Many were screaming. Some were badly burned. Witnesses called for ambulances. Others rushed to help.

When Herb Morrison finished his reporting, he and his engineer flew back to Chicago with the record discs that had captured his eyewitness account of this tragedy.

FACT FILE

Tragedy by the Numbers

Number of people aboard the *Hindenburg*: 97 (36 passengers and 61 crew members)

Number of people killed: 36 (13 passengers, 22 crew members, 1 ground crew member)

Number of survivors: 61 (23 passengers and 39 crew members)

The next day, Werner made his way back to the site where the *Hindenburg* had crashed. Amazingly, he had not been injured, but he had lost his most prized possession: the pocket watch his grandfather had given him. Combing through the charred debris, he searched and searched until he found it.

Investigators hunted for clues at the scene of the crash. They needed to find the cause of the disaster. Thirty-six people had died. So many more were injured. And the world was now hearing Herb's recording. Those who listened were horrified. How could the explosion have happened? The investigation ruled out sabotage, meaning someone having started the fire on purpose. Investigators suspected static electricity.

IMPACT ⚡

Cause

Decades after the disaster, a new investigation confirmed what caused that terrible explosion. Static electricity from the charged atmosphere ignited the flammable cover and leaking hydrogen. Almost everything else aboard also caught fire. This disaster quickly ended airship travel for passengers.

Journalism

Herb Morrison's report played around the world. It was the first time such a tragedy had been captured live by the media. It was shocking for audiences. Images of the explosion were quickly added to his audio recording, making the disaster even more awful for people to take in. After the groundbreaking recording of the *Hindenburg* disaster, the entire world knew Herb Morrison's name. He continued reporting and his coverage of the *Hindenburg* inspired more on-the-scene journalism.

AUTHOR'S NOTE

HELLO, fellow investigators!

You probably won't be surprised to learn that I was a curious and nosy kid. I loved finding out everything I could about anything happening in my home, neighborhood, town, and even in the world. And I also enjoyed telling everyone whatever I discovered. Sometimes that got me into trouble! But those traits came in handy when I decided to become an investigative reporter. That meant it was my job to find out all the information I could and tell the story of what I uncovered on the news. I loved it and even won a bunch of awards.

Now, after reading this book, you have had the chance to investigate some famous disasters and think about what you might have done in the situations described. You have been thinking about how these disasters happened and how things could have gone differently. Welcome to the club of curious minds that love finding out facts!

It's just the beginning for you. When you investigate the past, you are using detective skills that can be applied to the here and now, too. Clues and facts are all around us all the time. Now you know how to uncover the truth. You can ask important questions about an event, like who, what, where, when, how, and why? That's what real-life detectives, reporters, writers, historians, archaeologists, scientists, police officers, accident investigators, doctors, and others do every day. Speaking of questions, let's get to the most fun question of all: What will you investigate next?

SOURCE NOTES

Chapter 1: The Great Chicago Fire

p. 2: Everything was impossibly . . . ribbons of sand: Sewell, 18.

p. 4: "We are going . . . in my bones": quoted in Sheahan and Upton, 160.

p. 6: Ready for winter . . . tons of hay: "First Page of Handwritten Transcript of Catherine O'Leary's Testimony."

p. 6: *Fire! Fire! Fire!*: quoted in McDermott.

p. 8: Street call boxes . . . alerting them to the fire: Cooper, 40–41.

p. 9: Downtown, high atop . . . a spyglass: Darnell Little, "Box 342."

p. 10: The O'Learys' fire . . . fire department arrived: Cooper, 40–41.

p. 10: 185 full-time: ibid., 41.

p. 10: 11 alarm bells . . . throughout the city: Sheahan and Upton, 49.

p. 10: 88 horses: "Fire Figures."

p. 14: Dousing the flames . . . vital hose behind: Sheahan and Upton, 164.

p. 15: The fire started in the southern . . . at 20 miles per hour: Sawislak, 27–28.

p. 18: The gridlocked traffic . . . searched for them: Sewell, 32.

p. 19: "Come with us!": quoted in Otfinoski, 44.

p. 20: 400 feet: Cooper, 44.

p. 20: across the river: Regan, 23.

p. 21: the city's lanterns went dark: ibid.

p. 22: *Release all prisoners from jail at once*: quoted in Mason.

p. 22: "Run!": ibid.

p. 24: "This is the end of Chicago!": quoted in Bradwell.

p. 24: "No. No. She will rise again": ibid.

p. 25: He knew his fight was over: Sheahan and Upton, 169.

p. 26: Sometimes the air . . . creates a vacuum: Schmidt.

p. 26: if heated air rises . . . a fire tornado: "What Is a Firestorm?"

p. 28: On Monday evening, . . . a special edition: "The Great Calamity of the Age! Chicago in Ashes!!"

p. 29: One-third of . . . ash and ruins: Regan, 26.

p. 29: Total damage: $200 million . . . buildings destroyed: 18,000: Sewell, 17.

p. 29: Number left homeless . . . homes to survivors: ibid., 37.

p. 29: Undamaged railroad tracks . . . into the city quickly: Schons.

p. 29: a donation that made . . . first public library: ibid.

p. 30: "Don't worry, Judge . . . daughter is safe": quoted in Bradwell.

p. 31: "With the exception . . . in the world": quoted in Sewell, 45.

p. 37: Every year in . . . lessons learned from it: Cooper, 55.

Chapter 2: *Titanic*: Ship of Doom

p. 39: 9:30 a.m.: McPherson, 56.

p. 41: Captain Smith embarked . . . into another ship: ibid., 45–56.

pp. 42, 69: space for 1,178 people: Wells, 99.

p. 49: *Titanic* carried 5,892 tons . . . steam-powered engines: ibid., 6.

p. 50: Over the winter, . . . from glaciers: Wilkins.

p. 52: 386 miles: Wells, 74.

p. 52: 546 miles: Wells, 27, 74.

p. 53: The ice field . . . nautical miles: Maxtone-Graham, 30.

p. 55: This was cutting-edge . . . onshore operators: ibid., 1–23.

p. 56: *Icebergs and large quantities of field ice in 41°51′ N, 40°52′ W*: Milford.

p. 56: Around lunchtime, the telegraph machine stopped: Maxtone-Graham, 36.

p. 58: Wireless radio signals . . . were stronger and louder: Callery, *50 Things You Should Know about Titanic.*

p. 59: Shut up: quoted in McPherson, 27.

p. 61: "Iceberg right ahead!": ibid., 7.

p. 66: "So long, Frankie. I'll see you later": quoted in Goldsmith, 17.

p. 72: lifeboats pulled only forty people from the icy water: Kraterou.

Chapter 3: The Spanish Flu

p. 89: Keeping news about this deadly . . . they were facing: Becky Little, "As the 1918 Flu Emerged, Cover-Up and Denial Helped It Spread."

pp. 89–90: Meanwhile, in the Colorado town . . . Spanish influenza: Carroll.

p. 95: The flu virus would not be viewed . . . until the 1930s: Arnold, 7.

p. 99: "quarantine . . . against the world": quoted in Hanson.

p. 100: "The 'Flu' Is After Us" and "it is circulating . . . community around us": "The 'Flu' Is After Us."

p. 104: *I was a victim . . . am alright now*: Beatrice Williams.

p. 104: *It has been a contagious . . . died of it*: Griffin.

pp. 108–109: "Mama! Mama!," "Are you sick?" and "No, child. . . . as I could": quoted in "1918 Influenza Pandemic Survivor Interview: Mrs. Edna Boone, Interviewed 2008."

Chapter 4: The Boston Molasses Flood

p. 125: A cylinder made . . . place with rivets: Puleo, 11.

p. 126: The tank already had molasses . . . was still warm: ibid., 85.

p. 127: When cold molasses . . . carbon dioxide: ibid., 84.

p. 132: "bulging in and out": ibid., 70

p. 133: When pressure increases . . . until it fails: ibid., 70.

p. 134: 165 feet: ibid., 96.

p. 134: The sound of tearing metal . . . stopped the locomotive: Kops, 15.

p. 139: One of the workers . . . cause of the problems: Puleo, 71.

p. 141: Emergency workers from . . . free trapped victims: Kops, 35.

p. 143: "Huge molasses tank explodes!"; newspaper headline quoted in Puleo, 129.

Chapter 5: The Hindenburg

p. 154: 134 feet: Weber.

p. 156: When passengers lined up . . . claim these belongings: Majoor, 9.

p. 163: The *Hindenburg* was originally designed . . . could be used in war: Archbold, 144.

p. 164: "Well, here it comes . . . out of the sky": quoted in Archbold, 30.

p. 165: "Probably lining the . . . ahead of them": "Scenes From Hell."

p. 166: "It burst into flames!": ibid.

p. 166: "It is burning . . . all the passengers!": ibid.

p. 172: "This is the worst . . . I've ever witnessed": ibid.

BIBLIOGRAPHY

Adams, Tim. "The Big Picture: Spreading the Message about the 1918 Pandemic." *Guardian*, May 3, 2020. www.theguardian .com/artanddesign/2020/may/03/the-big-picture-spreading -the-message-about-the-1918-pandemic.

Allen, Phillip. "Teacher to End 63-Year Devotion." *Indianapolis News*, August 4, 1973, 5.

Archbold, Rick. *Hindenburg: An Illustrated History*. New York: Warner, 1994.

Arnold, Catharine. *Pandemic 1918: Eyewitness Accounts from the Greatest Medical Holocaust in Modern History*. New York: St. Martin's, 2018.

Associated Press. "Werner Franz, Survivor of *Hindenburg* Crash, Dies." NDTV.com, September 1, 2014. www.ndtv.com/world -news/werner-franz-survivor-of-hindenburg-crash-dies -657543.

Ballard, Robert D. *Titanic: Exploring the Discovery of a Lifetime*. Washington, DC: National Geographic, 2020.

Ballard, Robert D., and Nan Froman. *Finding the Titanic*. New York: Scholastic, 1993.

Botting, Douglas. *Dr. Eckener's Dream Machine: The Great Zeppelin and the Dawn of Air Travel*. New York: Henry Holt, 2002.

Bradwell, Bessie. "Bessie Bradwell." Excerpt from Bradwell's 1926 memoir. The Great Chicago Fire and the Web of Memory, Chicago History Museum and Northwestern University. www.greatchicagofire.org/anthology-of-fire-narratives /bessie-bradwell/.

Bromley, George Washington, and Walter Scott Bromley. "Atlas of the City of Boston, Boston Proper and Back Bay." Philadelphia: G. W. Bromley, 1922. https://ark.digitalcommonwealth .org/ark:/50959/9g54z693d.

Brown, Hallie Q. "Anna Elizabeth Hudlun." In *Homespun Heroines and Other Women of Distinction*, 141–144. Xenia, OH: Aldine, 1926. https://docsouth.unc.edu/neh/brownhal/brownhal .html.

Callery, Sean. *50 Things You Should Know about Titanic*. Lake Forest, CA: QED Publishing, 2016.

———. *Titanic: A Picture History of the Shipwreck That Shocked the World*. New York: Scholastic, 2014.

Carroll, Rory. "Gunnison, Colorado: The Town That Dodged the 1918 Spanish Flu Pandemic." *Guardian*, March 1, 2020. www .theguardian.com/world/2020/mar/01/gunnison-colorado -the-town-that-dodged-the-1918-spanish-flu-pandemic.

City of Westfield, Indiana. "Why the Name Armstrong Park?" www.westfield.in.gov/egov/documents/1347377762_92497 .html.

Cooper, Michael L. *Fighting Fire! Ten of the Deadliest Fires in American History and How We Fought Them*. New York: Henry Holt, 2014.

"COSI Interview with Tom Goldsmith, Grandson of *Titanic* Survivor." Interview by COSI Science Center of Columbus, Ohio, April 14, 2010. https://youtu.be/LYhjDdSIODA.

Coughlan, Sean. "*Titanic*: The Final Messages from a Stricken Ship." BBC News, April 10, 2012. http://www.bbc.com/news /magazine-17631595.

"David A. Anderson Dies at Camp Dix, New Jersey." *Gunnison News-Champion*, September 27, 1918, 1.

"Dear Sergeant Teacher: World War I Letters to Irven Armstrong." *Black History News and Notes*, August 2001. https://images .indianahistory.org/digital/collection/p16797coll66/id/21.

Durr, Eric. "Worldwide Flu Outbreak Killed 45,000 American Soldiers during World War I." US Army, August 31, 2018. www.army.mil/article/210420/worldwide_flu_outbreak _killed_45000_american_soldiers_during_world_war_i.

"Early Chicago: The Great Fire." In "DuSable to Obama: Chicago's Black Metropolis." WTTW, August 16, 2018. https://interactive.wttw.com/dusable-to-obama/the-great-fire.

Engber, Daniel. "Black Smoke over Beirut: Why Isn't It White?" *Slate*, July 17, 2006. slate.com/news-and-politics/2006/07 /where-does-black-smoke-come-from.html.

Ewing, E. Thomas. "Flu Masks Failed in 1918, but We Need Them Now." Health Affairs, May 12, 2020. www.healthaffairs.org /do/10.1377/hblog20200508.769108/full/.

"Fire Figures." The Great Chicago Fire and the Web of Memory, Chicago Historical Society and Northwestern University. https://www.greatchicagofire.org/timeline/item/1871-04-11/.

"First Page of Handwritten Transcript of Catherine O'Leary's Testimony before the Board of Police and Fire Commissioners, 1871." The Great Chicago Fire and the Web of Memory, Chicago Historical Society and Northwestern University. https://www.greatchicagofire.org/item/ichi-32210/.

"The 'Flu' Is After Us." *Gunnison News-Champion*, October 10, 1918. chm.med.umich.edu/wp-content/uploads /sites/20/2015/02/gnc03.pdf.

Folkart, Burt A. "Herbert Morrison; Radio Reporter at *Hindenburg* Crash." *Los Angeles Times*, January 11, 1989. www.latimes .com/archives/la-xpm-1989-01-11-mn-31-story.html.

Gamble, Vanessa Northington. "'There Wasn't a Lot of Comforts in Those Days': African Americans, Public Health, and the 1918 Influenza Epidemic." *Public Health Reports* 125, suppl. 3 (July–August 2010): 114–122. https://www.ncbi.nlm.nih.gov /pmc/articles/PMC2862340/.

Goldsmith, Frank J. W. *Titanic Eyewitness: My Story*. Indian Orchard, MA: Titanic Historical Society, 2007.

"The Great Boston Molasses Flood of 1919." New England Historical Society, January 15, 2020. www.newenglandhistorical society.com/great-boston-molasses-disaster-1919/.

"The Great Calamity of the Age! Chicago in Ashes!!" *Chicago Evening Journal*, October 9, 1871.

Griffin, Earlee A., to Irven Armstrong. Letter, November 7, 1918. Irven Armstrong Collection, 1918–1996, Indiana Historical Society. https://images.indianahistory.org/digital/collection /dc042/id/238/rec/4.

Grossman, Dan. "*Hindenburg* Design and Technology." Airships. net. www.airships.net/hindenburg/hindenburg-design -technology/.

———. "The *Hindenburg* Disaster." Airships.net. www.airships .net/hindenburg/disaster/.

Hannoun, Claude. "The Evolving History of Influenza Viruses and Vaccines." *Expert Review of Vaccines* 12, no. 9 (2013): 1085–1094. www.medscape.com/viewarticle/812621_1.

Hanson, F. P. "Quarantine Proclamation by the County Physician." *Gunnison News-Champion*, November 1, 1918. https://quod .lib.umich.edu/f/flu/2540flu.0014.452/1/flu-toll-is-terrific.

History.com editors. "World War I." History.com, October 29, 2009. www.history.com/topics/world-war-i/world-war-i -history.

Hobday, Richard A., and John W. Cason. "The Open-Air Treatment of Pandemic Influenza." *American Journal of Public Health* 99 (October 2009): S236–S242. https://ajph.aphapublications .org/doi/10.2105/AJPH.2008.134627.

Hopkinson, Deborah. *Titanic: Voices from the Disaster.* New York: Scholastic, 2012.

"Interview with Irven Armstrong, Teacher at Crispus Attucks High School, Conducted April 6, 1977." Joseph T. Taylor Papers, 1922–2000, Indiana Historical Society. https://images.indiana history.org/digital/collection/p16797coll34/id/27.

Klein, Christopher. "Why October 1918 Was America's Deadliest Month Ever." History.com, October 5, 2018. www.history.com /news/spanish-flu-deaths-october-1918.

Kops, Deborah. *The Great Molasses Flood: Boston, 1919.* Watertown, MA: Charlesbridge, 2015.

Kraterou, Aliki. "Documentary Reveals the Private Journal of Judge Who Investigated *Titanic* Disaster." *Daily Mail Online*, updated January 5, 2021. https://www.dailymail.co.uk/news /article-9110827/Documentary-reveals-private-journal -judge-investigated-Titanic-disaster.html.

Little, Becky. "As the 1918 Flu Emerged, Cover-Up and Denial Helped It Spread." History.com, May 26, 2020. www.history .com/news/1918-pandemic-spanish-flu-censorship.

———. "When Mask-Wearing Rules in the 1918 Pandemic Faced Resistance." History.com, May 6, 2020. www.history.com /news/1918-spanish-flu-mask-wearing-resistance.

Little, Darnell. "Box 342." *Chicago Tribune*, November 9, 1996. https://www.chicagotribune.com/news/ct-xpm-1996-11-09 -9701150581-story.html.

————. "Dead Cows Tell No Tales." *Chicago Tribune*, November 9, 1996. www.chicagotribune.com/news/ct-xpm-1996-11-09 -9701150573-story.html.

Majoor, Mireille. *Inside the Hindenburg*. Toronto: McArthur, 2000.

Malcolm, Andrew H. "*Titanic* Survivor Joins a Lost Father." *New York Times*, April 16, 1982. http://www.nytimes .com/1982/04/16/us/titanic-survivor-joins-a-lost-father.html.

Marriott, Leo. *Titanic*. New York: Smithmark, 1997.

Mason, Roswell. "Mayor Roswell Mason Note Ordering the Release of Prisoners, October 9, 1871." The Great Chicago Fire and the Web of Memory, Chicago Historical Society and Northwestern University. www.greatchicagofire.org /great-conflagration/inside-burning-city/.

Maxtone-Graham, John. *Titanic Tragedy: A New Look at the Lost Liner*. New York: Norton, 2012.

McDermott, Michael. "How It Originated." *Chicago Tribune*, October 20, 1871, 2.

McPherson, Stephanie Sammartino. *Iceberg Right Ahead! The Tragedy of the Titanic*. Minneapolis: Twenty-First Century, 2012.

Milford, Joshua Allen. "Ice Warning Five." *Titanic*: History's Most Famous Ship. www.jmilford-titanic.com/2014/08/april-14 -1912-ice-warning-five.html.

"1918 Influenza Pandemic Survivor Interview: Mrs. Edna Boone, Interviewed 2008." Interviewed January 28, 2008, by Ann Brantley. Alabama Department of Archives and History, August 27, 2012. https://youtu.be/7k20VFZeLKY.

Noon, Steve, and Eric Kentley. *Story of the Titanic*. New York: Dorling Kindersley, 2001.

O'Donnell, E. E. *The Last Days of the Titanic: Photographs and Mementos of the Tragic Maiden Voyage.* Niwot, CO: Roberts Rinehart, 1997.

Otfinoski, Steven. *The Great Chicago Fire: All Is Not Lost.* Mankato, MN: Capstone, 2019.

Park, Edwards. "Without Warning, Molasses Surged over Boston 100 Years Ago." *Smithsonian*, November 1983. http://www .smithsonianmag.com/history/without-warning-molasses -january-surged-over-boston-180971251.

Puleo, Stephen. *Dark Tide: The Great Boston Molasses Flood of 1919.* Boston: Beacon, 2019.

Regan, Michael. *The Great Chicago Fire: A Cause-and-Effect Investigation.* Minneapolis: Lerner, 2017.

Russell, Patrick. "Werner Franz." *Faces of the Hindenburg* (blog), September 29, 2009. facesofthehindenburg.blogspot .com/2009/09/werner-franz.html.

Sangiacomo, Michael. "*Titanic* 100th Anniversary: Thomas Goldsmith's Grandfather Survived, but Couldn't Discuss Sinking." Cleveland.com, April 8, 2012. http:// www.cleveland.com/metro/index.ssf/2012/04/titanic_100th _anniversary_thom.html.

Sawislak, Karen. *Smoldering City: Chicagoans and the Great Fire, 1871–1874.* Chicago: University of Chicago Press, 1995.

"Scenes From Hell." *Eyewitness: American Originals from the National Archives*, National Archives and Records Administration. https://www.archives.gov/exhibits/eyewitness/html.php ?section=5.

Schmidt, Amanda. "How Destructive Wildfires Create Their Own Weather." AccuWeather. www.accuweather.com/en/weather -news/how-destructive-wildfires-create-their-own-weather /346337.

Schons, Mary. "The Chicago Fire of 1871 and the 'Great Rebuilding.'" *National Geographic*, January 25, 2011. https://www .nationalgeographic.org/article/chicago-fire-1871-and-great -rebuilding/.

Schudel, Matt. "Werner Franz, One of the Last Survivors of the 1937 *Hindenburg* Crash, Dies at 92." *Washington Post*, August 30, 2014. www.washingtonpost.com/world/werner-franz -one-of-the-last-survivors-of-the-1937-hindenburg-crash-dies -at-92/2014/08/30/e85eaf36-3053-11e4-9b98-848790384093 _story.html.

Sewell, Alfred L. *"The Great Calamity!" Scenes, Incidents, and Lessons of the Great Chicago Fire*. Chicago: Alfred L. Sewell, 1871.

Sheahan, James W., and George P. Upton. *The Great Conflagration: Chicago, Its Past, Present and Future*. Chicago: Union Publishing, 1872.

"Smoke Color Can Depict Fuel Type." RedZone, January 23, 2016. www.redzone.co/2016/01/23/smoke-color-can-depict-fuel -type/.

"Spanish Flu Close By." *Gunnison News-Champion*, October 11, 1918, 1.

Stewart, Melissa. *Titanic*. Washington, DC: National Geographic, 2012.

University of Michigan Center for the History of Medicine. "Gunnison." chm.med.umich.edu/research/1918-influenza -escape-communities/gunnison/.

Weber, Bruce. "Werner Franz, Survivor of the *Hindenburg*'s Crew, Dies at 92." *New York Times*, August 30, 2014. www.nytimes .com/2014/08/31/world/europe/werner-franz-survivor-of -the-hindenburgs-crew-dies-at-92.html.

Wells, Susan. *Titanic: Legacy of the World's Greatest Ocean Liner*. New York: Time Life Education, 1997.

"What Is a Firestorm?" National Oceanic and Atmospheric Administration SciJinks. Last modified August 6, 2021. www.scijinks .gov/firestorm/.

Wilkins, Alasdair. "What Happened to the Iceberg That Sank the *Titanic?*" *Wired*, April 16, 2012. www.wired.com/2012/04 /titanic-iceberg-history/.

Williams, Beatrice, to Irven Armstrong. Letter, November 7, 1918. Irven Armstrong Collection, 1918–1996, Indiana Historical Society. https://images.indianahistory.org/digital/collection /dc042/id/32/rec/2.

Woodruff, Andy. "Mapping Molasses." Bostonography, January 15, 2019. https:// www.bostonography.com/2019/mapping -molasses/.

INDEX

Page numbers in *italics* indicate illustrations.